CLASH *of* EAGLES

Lieutenant William Francis Lynch commanded America's 1848 naval expedition to Palestine. *Courtesy of the Library of Congress*

CLASH *of* EAGLES

America's Forgotten Expedition
to Ottoman Palestine

Carol Lea Clark

Lyons Press
Guilford, Connecticut
An imprint of Globe Pequot Press

All images are from William Lynch's *Narrative of the United States' Expedition to
the River Jordan and the Dead Sea* unless otherwise noted.

Endpapers: The 1848 American naval expedition created this map of Palestine.
The members of the expedition used sextants and chronometers to determine
latitude and longitude, and their training in topological drawing enabled them
to fill in many previously unrecorded curves and gaps. Map courtesy of the
Library of Congress.

Frontispiece: Lieutenant William Francis Lynch commanded America's 1848
naval expedition to Palestine. Courtesy of the Library of Congress

Library of Congress Cataloging-in-Publication Data is available on file.

ISBN 978-0-7627-7842-3

Printed in the United States of America

10 9 8 7 6 5 4 3 2 1

To my father, the late Morris L. Usry,
who introduced me to the world of nineteenth-century exploration
and who would have loved to read this book.

Where'er we tread 'tis haunted, holy ground.

—LORD BYRON,
CHILDE HAROLD'S PILGRIMAGE

CONTENTS

I

Arrival

The USS *Supply* battled strong winds and stronger waves in the eastern Mediterranean as it sailed past the ports of Sidon, Tyre, and Acre. At midnight, the ship's white canvases shivered in the faint moonlight as the crew shortened sails on the three masts. Then the helmsman turned the ship into the wind, and the crew dropped anchor below Mount Carmel at Haifa, a walled village in Ottoman Palestine.

The *Supply*, a square-rigged vessel of 556 metric tons, had been commissioned in 1846 for the Mexican-American War. Her name reveals her original mission: to replenish American warships wherever need arose around the world. Rather than an ungainly workhorse of a store ship, though, the *Supply* was sleek, capable of 11.5 knots—swift for a square rigged vessel.[1] She would have been a pleasure to maneuver.

The USS *Supply*, which Lynch sailed from New York Harbor to Acre to deliver the men and supplies for the Palestine expedition. Painting by W. R. May, possibly in the 1870s. *Courtesy of the Naval War College Museum.*

Under the command of Lieutenant William Francis Lynch, she had begun her journey four months before in the Brooklyn Navy Yard on Friday, November 20, 1847, dropping down near the Battery in New York Harbor to await a west-northwest wind favorable for an Atlantic crossing. For the *Supply* headed not to enemy waters off Mexico but east to the Mediterranean.[2] She made landfall first at Gibraltar, then stopped at Port Mahon on Minorca in the Balearics to replenish America's Mediterranean fleet. Lynch headed east again, stopping at Smyrna, Constantinople, and Beirut. By the time it reached Haifa, the *Supply* had sailed a quarter of the way around the world to bring Lynch, three other officers, two volunteers—including Lynch's son, Francis—a physician-naturalist, and a complement of nine sailors on the official American naval expedition to map the Dead Sea.

At first light, the masthead lookout could see pale purple hills rising from the water in the east, then the curved shoreline of the bay, and finally the fishing boats swinging fitfully at anchor. After full daylight, irresistibly drawn by the prospect of setting foot on the sacred soil of Palestine, Lynch ignored his own weakened health from a case of smallpox he had contracted in Gibraltar only weeks before. He also disregarded the strong wind and heavy surf and attempted to land a small boat on the beach near Haifa. As he later wrote, he experienced great difficulty getting the ship's boat to shore. It was a laughable understatement, for storm waves off the coast of Palestine can reach heights in excess of fifteen feet for as long as fifteen seconds, and even shorter waves herald longer-than-normal swells—hardly suitable conditions for landing a small boat.[3]

Lynch, along with a US vice consul to the Ottoman Empire, who had accompanied him from Beirut, almost died before the expedition could begin. The boat taking them ashore capsized. Wearing his bulky wool uniform, boots, and sword, Lynch suffered baptism by salt water in the heavy surf. He would have wondered, floundering underwater—fighting the current and the waves, clawing for the light and the air above—if he was going to die so close to the Promised Land. Local Arab fishermen spotted the two men slip beneath the waves and dived into the water to pull them, dripping and gasping, to safety. Lynch gratefully described the fishermen as bold, lithe swimmers, as much at home in the water as Lynch had observed the natives of the

Sandwich Islands to be.[4] Which Lynch, like many Navy men oddly enough, was not.

But this was hardly his first brush with death. When he was a midshipman, a shortage of water forced his ship to anchor off cholera-infested Manila. Lynch and his shipmates felt helpless in the face of the disease, which people then believed was transmitted through the air. He wrote, "The pestilence [was] stealthily gliding on the water . . . born by sickly airs from the land, and enveloped us in its folds, one by one garnered its victims." As soon as they could, they sailed, taking the disease with them, and the pestilence festered until no one was able to man the ship and the cries begging for water had no one healthy to respond. Lynch awoke in his shipboard hammock from a stupor to find that the six men around him had died during the night. The ship lost more than seventy men to the disease.[5]

Moreover, he suffered from a mysterious illness himself that may have been tuberculosis; earlier, it had forced him to take a two-year leave of absence from his duties for treatment and compelled him to avoid winter postings altogether.[6] Lynch's close acquaintance with death caused him, very much a man of his age, not to crave safety but to rush forward into danger. He sought command of the perilous Palestine expedition that might cause his death far from home, bringing him both everlasting peace and everlasting glory. The expedition might also save his eternal soul, a concern of deep significance in fire-and-brimstone antebellum America. Walking where Christ had walked would bring him closer to a blessed afterlife. If nothing else, it would help him understand the contrasts of the violent and vengeful Old Testament God of his childhood and the forgiving love of the New Testament Jesus that soon would become the prevailing

belief in late nineteenth-century America. Likewise, the mission could leave a lasting legacy by fostering closer ties with the Holy Land.

Seawater soaked his officer's uniform of blue wool with eagle-studded brass buttons, but, with the help of those bold and lithe fishermen, Lynch managed to get ashore with his sword still at his side. Until the surf calmed, he was cut off from the ship, so he took refuge with the monks of Mount Carmel, their monastery and church sprawled on the broad bluff overlooking the ocean. For two days, waiting for the sea to moderate, he shared the monks' vegetarian fare and spartan quarters above a grotto where the prophet Elijah was believed to have lived.

Though the Carmelite Order traces its history on Mount Carmel to the prophets Elijah and Elisha, historians date the origin to the middle of the twelfth century when a community of men lived there, dedicating their lives to God's service. But Mount Carmel was considered sacred long before, even into prehistoric times, a high place visible, as it is, for great distances. By the third or fourth century, pilgrims traveled to Mount Carmel to worship at Elijah's grotto. The Carmelite Order flourished, becoming a major order of the Catholic Church, but its home in Palestine did not fare as well. After the Mamluk Dynasty conquest of Palestine in 1291, the Carmelites were expelled, though a branch of the order returned in 1631. Under Islamic rule, the monastery became a mosque. Napoleon used it as a hospital in 1799, and in 1821 Abdallah Pasha of Damascus ordered it destroyed. In 1838, the Carmelites began constructing a new monastery and basilica, which is where Lynch took refuge.

An ambitious, curly-haired, slender man of forty-six, with a high, intellectual forehead and a deceptively frail

appearance, Lynch would have taken the weather-ordained respite to review the events that brought him to Haifa. As a midshipman, during the voyage of the USS *Congress* to South America and China, he had developed a taste for exploration. Then, while on leave after his return to the United States, he experienced a dramatic dream of Judgment Day, envisioning himself sitting at the feet of Jesus, watching the judging of individuals from the beginning of time to the present day. These two pivotal experiences may have set him on the trajectory that led him to the present moment in the Holy Land, about to explore the Dead Sea, the site of Sodom and the Cities of the Plain, the recipients of God's wrath at their citizens' refusal to repent of their sins.[7]

He acquired command of the Palestine expedition by asking astutely at perhaps the one moment the request would be granted. In 1847, the United States was embroiled in the Mexican-American War, but the navy played only a minor role in the hostilities, ferrying army troops into the Gulf of Mexico to capture the town and castle of Vera Cruz, marching inland from there toward Mexico City. In his proposal to John Mason, secretary of the navy, Lynch strategically devalued the navy's role in the war, indicating that there was "nothing left for the Navy to perform."[8] He suggested the Dead Sea cartography mission as an opportunity for the navy to garner favorable publicity, knowing that Mason had a reputation for supporting scientific expeditions.[9]

Secretary Mason agreed. The army had garnered laudatory headlines after its victories in the war, while the navy essentially went unnoticed in the press. He wrote to Lynch confidentially that the object of the expedition was "to promote the cause of Sciences, and advance the character of the Naval

Secretary of the Navy John Mason, who authorized the
expedition, and after whose daughter the expedition named
their copper boat the *Fanny Mason*. *Courtesy of the Navy
Historical Collection.*

service; to accomplish which a more favorable opportunity
will probably not occur."[10] In other words, though Secretary
Mason might welcome the mission's scientific accomplishments, the trip was primarily a publicity stunt.

That said, the mission's objectives were not entirely unreasonable, given the recent worldwide expansion of American commerce. In 1830, President Andrew Jackson and Sultan Mahmud II signed an American-Ottoman friendship treaty that allowed for trading privileges and the right of American ships to call at Ottoman ports. However, America still lagged behind Britain and various European nations in establishing a trading presence in the Middle East, partially because its primary interests were in the Americas, but also because the United States would have to develop its own exclusive trade route to compete for the commerce of the Ottoman Empire and the Far East.[11]

From the fall of the Crusader Kingdom in 1291 until the end of the eighteenth century, none of the world's major powers cared much about the region. What Christian groups remained turned into insignificant and "tiny islands in a hostile sea" while European powers busily colonized other continents or fought each other.[12] In 1516, though, France made a treaty with the Ottoman Empire, which granted it the right to "protect" the holy sites, a privilege immediately contested by other Catholic countries. However, the growth of Protestantism delayed interest in pilgrimages to the Holy Land, as doctrine emphasized journeys of the spirit rather than physical pilgrimages.

Even Ottoman sultans showed little interest in the region, for only meager revenue flowed from the poverty-level, ethnically mixed population into their coffers in Istanbul. They regarded the holy places as nuisances because of the religious fanatics that they attracted, the most troubling from Orthodox Russia. The few Western European or American foreigners who traveled to the region most often described Palestine at the time as a "backwater" of a dying empire.[13]

But in 1799, Napoleon refocused the attention of Europe to this part of the world by taking a page from the book of Alexander the Great and invading it. Though his Middle East campaign ultimately failed, he made Britain and other major European countries reexamine the security of their trade routes through the Middle East, causing them slowly to realize that unrest in Palestine left them vulnerable. Britain, especially, after the loss of the American colonies, had become dependent upon trade with India and the Far East, which flowed through the Middle East.

In 1831, Muhammad[14] Ali Pasha of Egypt and his adopted son, Ibrahim Pasha, further destabilized the situation in the Middle East, at least from the European powers' perspective, when they fought with their Ottoman overlords and, in the process, occupied Palestine for nine years. Understandably fearing the collapse of the Ottoman Empire and the vacuum of power it would create, Britain and other European nations intervened and returned Palestine to Ottoman control. However, this benevolence toward the Ottomans came with a price, and the European nations began to take control of the holy places such as the Church of the Holy Sepulcher. The British in particular began to consider alternative overland trade routes to India and the Far East.

One such alternative was a canal. Napoleon's archaeologists and other scientists had searched for evidence of an ancient Suez canal, and they published their findings in the *Description de l'Egypte*, documenting an ancient canal from the Red Sea to the Nile. But his surveyors discounted the possibility of constructing a canal from the Red Sea to the Mediterranean, claiming that the levels of the two bodies of water differed by ten meters. British explorer and artillery officer Francis Rawdon Chesney, though, discovered

the French error and wrote a report in 1830 detailing the feasibility of a canal at Suez, though decades passed before anyone attempted its construction.[15] Chesney went on to explore and advocate a new overland trade route to the east that used steamships on the Euphrates River, which he tested in an expedition in 1836. He proved the Euphrates to be navigable, which earned him a gold medal from the Royal Geographical Society, though the route never became popular.

At the time of the American Palestine expedition in 1848, the perception of the strategic importance of Palestine's location at the crossroads between the West and the East, on the part of the European powers and the United States, or at least any implementation of a change in perception, was slowly increasing. But then an increased appreciation for the Holy Land, as crucial to Protestantism, added momentum.

In 1841, the celebrated American professor of theology Edward Robinson, sometimes called the father of biblical geography, published *Biblical Researches in Palestine, Mount Sinai, and Arabia Petraea*. The book influenced many, including Lynch, with its vivid descriptions of the Palestinian landscape, including the Jordan River and the Dead Sea.

Robinson, like Lynch, had a restless spirit that hadn't been content with the opportunities available near home, which in his case was a farm in Southington, Connecticut. He became a brilliant classics scholar, first at Hamilton College in upstate New York, then at Andover Theological Seminary in Massachusetts, followed by a stint in Europe, studying Hebrew scripture for four years with scholars such as Silvestre de Sacy and Wilhelm Gesenius. Robinson returned to America to teach at Andover and founded an academic journal, *The American Bible Repository*, which promoted a conservative agenda by defending the Bible's literal accuracy. By 1837, many considered him one of the most outstanding biblical scholars in America, and he was named the first chair of biblical literature at the Union Theological Seminary in New York. He accepted the appointment but delayed taking up residence so that he could spend several years studying in Palestine.

With Eli Smith, an Arabic-speaking missionary based in Beirut, Robinson set off on his version of an Old Testament reenactment. Starting his tour in Egypt, he followed the route of the ancient Israelites across the Sinai, then into Palestine, past the Dead Sea, north to Jerusalem, and on to Beirut. During the trip, Robinson kept detailed notes, which he turned into a landmark book lauded on both sides of the Atlantic. In 1842, the Royal Geographical Society in London, that bastion of "scientific" exploration, awarded its gold medal to Robinson, the first American to receive the honor.[16]

As Lynch would do so later, Robinson connected the Palestine landscape with biblical events. In Bi res-Seba', known in the Bible as Beersheba, he reflected in his journal, "Here is the place where the Patriarchs Abraham, Isaac and Jacob often dwelt!" In Jerusalem, Robinson applied his knowledge of the writings of Josephus Flavius, first-century Jewish historian, to identify odd-shaped stones projecting from the Harim wall, which others had supposed were caused by an earthquake, as the remains of an entrance arch to the temple built by Herod. In the countryside, assisted by Smith, Robinson compared the Arabic

names for Palestinian villages to locations mentioned in the ancient Hebrew of the Old Testament and identified dozens of biblical locations.[17]

The part of Robinson's book that most immediately interested Lynch, though, was the suggestion of a trade route through Palestine via the Jordan Valley, which bisected the region from Lake Hula, north of the Sea of Galilee, to the Gulf of Aqaba. After reading the book and talking with its author, Lynch became intrigued by the idea of finding a trade route across Palestine down the Jordan River and through the Dead Sea, to the Red Sea and the Indian Ocean. At the time, no one had shown that the Dead Sea was navigable, though an Irishman named Christopher Costigan, with a Maltese sailing companion, had tried to sail it in 1835. Unfortunately, it was midsummer. Adrift in a small boat under the scorching, relentless sun, Costigan lost consciousness, though his companion was able to get the boat to shore and summon help from Jericho. Costigan died two days later in Jerusalem from heatstroke complicated by the effects of drinking Dead Sea water after running out of fresh water in the unremitting heat.

In 1847, Lieutenant William Molyneux headed a British Navy expedition that tried floating down the Jordan River from the Sea of Galilee to the Dead Sea. Again, the weather went against them, and they also suffered from sunstroke, making them easy prey. Marauding Bedouin forced Molyneux to pay tribute to avoid attack. He became separated from his crew and feared they had been attacked by Bedouin—which they had. He died during an agonizing search for them in the intense August heat. Lynch took the deaths of the two previous expedition commanders not as a cautionary tale but as a challenge. He believed that Yankee ingenuity could succeed where men of other nations had failed. Americans could learn from others' mistakes. They would sail the Dead Sea and determine if the Jordan River to the Dead Sea to the Red Sea was a viable trade route.

Though not totally far-fetched, the expedition plan looks curious when compared to other exploring expeditions. Perplexed by the anomaly of the expedition, historian David Finnie suggests that Lynch simply had a "bee in his bonnet" and managed to persuade Secretary Mason to authorize what Finnie called an "utterly unpolitical" expedition.[18]

But another motivation may have inspired Lynch: to establish a symbolic American presence in the Holy Land by traversing the landscape, flying the American flag in the midst of the Dead Sea. This purpose aligned with America's belief in Manifest Destiny—which many in the nineteenth century envisioned as expanding the American nation farther than merely the Atlantic to the Pacific—and Secretary Mason might have tacitly supported Lynch's symbolic empirialism. The progress of the United States was preordained, many Americans believed, and it was America's destiny to assume a preeminent place in the community of nations. America was God's new chosen country, and Lynch hoped the expedition would firmly establish an American stake in Palestine, God's original Promised Land.

On October 2, 1847, Lynch received orders to report to the Brooklyn Navy Yard to take command of the *Supply*. He was to choose a crew for the expedition and assemble the necessary equipment. Lynch ordered two custom metal boats to be built, more durable than wooden boats, to traverse the rapids of the Jordan River, and they were constructed so that they could, if necessary, be taken apart in eight pieces, with each piece strapped to the back of a camel or mule, though Lynch hoped to transport the boats intact. Both boats would fly the American flag, then featuring twenty-nine white stars as well as the usual thirteen red and white stripes. Extra flags stood at the ready to mark Palestine territory with the American presence.

The stores included an impressive array of armaments in anticipation of violence in the lawless wilds. The expedition was armed to the teeth. Lynch and the other officers wore special swords with built-in rifle barrels, and the enlisted men carried pistols that also featured foot-long bowie knife blades. Both weapons allowed for ship-to-ship boarding, in which the rifle or pistol could be fired once at a distance before the blades were used in close, hand-to-hand battle. The expedition also had Colt revolvers and carbines. A buck-shot-firing blunderbuss, an early version of a shotgun, with a large and impressively flared muzzle, could be mounted on a base for stability. The boats had even been modified to include a support for it, to discourage any attack as they were going downriver.

Lynch selected as officers Lieutenant John B. Dale, who prepared the expedition's maps with Passed Midshipman Richmond Aulick; and Joseph C. Thomas, master's mate and armorer. Francis Edward Lynch, Lynch's son, had charge of the herbarium. Henry J. Anderson, M.D., also a geologist, came aboard at Beirut and Henry Bedlow, Esq., also a volunteer, joined at Istanbul. Nine enlisted seamen completed the American crew.

Despite Secretary Mason's positive reaction to Lynch's proposal of a Palestine expedition, the idea did not immediately captivate the American press. The *New York Herald's* headline just before the *Supply* sailed, read: "Interesting

After Iowa's admission to the Union, the twenty-nine-star version of the flag became official on July 4, 1847, and lasted for one year. From 1845 to 1867, Union forces often flew flags with this star arrangement, known as the Diamond Pattern. *Created by Gunter Küchler, courtesy Wikimedia Commons.*

Naval Intelligence: A Curious Expedition," and devoted just thirteen lines of type to explain that the *Supply* would sail "for the purpose of making an exploration and survey of the Dead Sea. . . . What object is intended, other than scientific research, we cannot at present say."[19]

Lynch, feeling defensive, sent a lengthy letter to the editor of the *Herald* that argued that the mission would serve the interests of science and religion both. The expedition would reveal by scientific means "the visitation of God's wrath." He also pointed out that Britain had sent two expeditions that had "failed in a like attempt," implying that the Americans might succeed where the British had failed, besting their former colonial overlords. Lynch's letter appeared in the *Herald* on November 23, the day that prevailing winds changed and the *Supply* was able to sail east on its voyage.

The expedition's blunderbuss, a mounted rifle-like weapon with a wide muzzle to scatter shot at close range.

Anyone reading the exchange who understood geography, though, would have realized that the expedition was more audacious than curious. For the past ten years, British and European explorers had been racing to prove what was suspected but not yet conclusively established: that the Dead Sea lay below sea level. No less than five groups of gentlemen geographers, some considered top scientists in Europe, had visited the sea for periods varying from several hours to several weeks. Though equipped with an array of scientific instruments ranging from basic thermometers to the era's most sophisticated barometers, they experienced equipment failures or human error in computations. In all cases, these eminent men had failed to prove the level of the Dead Sea to the satisfaction of the Royal Geographical Society and similar scientific organizations in Europe.[20]

Coincidentally, just four days before the *Supply* weighed anchor in the Brooklyn Navy Yard, Edward Robinson—who had speculated about a trade route through Palestine—had delivered a stirring address to the Royal Geographical Society in London, urging members of that illustrious group "that they, who have it in their power, will speedily . . . venture once again to the Dead Sea to settle the issue" of its level.[21]

But why was it so important to nineteenth-century researchers to prove that the Dead Sea lay below sea level? Many scientists of the era believed that the geography of Palestine was biblical testament that spoke to the accuracy of statements made by Moses and the prophets, indeed, to the inerrancy of Jewish and therefore Christian Scripture. In this, they were countering the growing numbers of revisionists who viewed the Bible as a flawed and inconsistent document. In no way did it compromise the rigor of their science, they argued, to search for biblical truths. Indeed, "proving" the Bible would unite their two essential beliefs—in science and in God. If the Dead Sea proved to lie below sea level, it would mean that Sodom and the other Cities of the Plain had suffered a monumental cataclysm, as the Bible describes, that had rendered the region unique on Earth.

It didn't bother Lynch that he wasn't a gentleman in the sense of being born to moneyed aristocracy. In Britain and

Europe, that status was practically a prerequisite for being recognized as an eminent scientist, though there were a few notable exceptions such as Michael Faraday, who conducted landmark experiments in electromagnetism. The majority of the members of the Royal Geographical Society had high social standing: Dukes, earls, and baronets were geographers, geologists, natural philosophers, astronomers, and military officers. If those scientists weren't titled already, many lusted for knighthood as a reward for their efforts.

But Lynch was American, one of God's new chosen people, proud of the egalitarian heritage that allowed him to rise from the ranks based on his own ability and hard work. His training as a naval officer, as well as his own studies in geography, botany, geology, and history, qualified him to conduct scientific research in Palestine. If his expedition proved the Dead Sea did lie below sea level, it would demonstrate that Americans could compete on the world stage along with the best scientists the Old World could offer.

Traumatic events in his personal life doubtless intensified the urgency of this quest for Lynch. The previous October, he had received compassionate leave because of the death of his daughter, Mary Virginia, at age eighteen, leaving him with sixteen-year-old son, Francis, as his only surviving child. To make matters worse, he was suing his wife for divorce, alleging "wanton" acts that a relative identified in court as adultery. A surviving letter from Lynch's best friend, Matthew Fontaine Maury, to a cousin discloses knowledge not public at the time—that the infidelity was with one of Lynch's brothers, Edward or Eugene. Both brothers died in 1843, perhaps from tuberculosis, an illness that also may have plagued Lynch. The painful divorce proceedings dragged on, however, and were not completed until after his return from Palestine.

Feeling reborn after his near drowning in the surf, Lynch rejoiced in the fulfillment of a closely held dream of twenty years to visit the Promised Land. So often, he had fantasized about the Holy Land, imagining what it would be like to tread the same landscape as had Jesus Christ. *What would it feel like to mingle with residents dressed in flowing robes and,* he thought, *living much the same as had the farmers, fishermen, and merchants in biblical times?*

Waiting for the storm to pass, when he could unload his men and the expedition's boats, as well as turn over temporary command of the *Supply,* he enjoyed the magnificent view of Palestine from the summit of Mount Carmel. The massive headland of a twenty-four-mile mountain range, Mount Carmel extends into the Mediterranean and, rising to a height of 1,700 feet, forms part of the huge crescent-shaped bay that extends from Haifa to Acre. Lynch recorded his impression of the view: "Beneath Mt. Carmel is a narrow but luxuriant plain. Sweeping inland, north and south with Acre in the near perspective, are the hills of Samaria and Galilee, enclosing the lovely vale of Sharon, while to the west lies the broad expanse of the Mediterranean."[22]

The Palestine that Lynch observed from Mount Carmel was not a country, nor had it been one since Old Testament times. It was not even a province of the Ottoman Empire as it had been in the late Roman Empire. What Christians considered biblical Palestine—from the Mediterranean to the Jordan River and from Dan to Beersheba—composed parts of several Ottoman *eyaltes* or provinces. The Ottomans saw no advantages in creating a single administrative unit called "Palestine" out of what was, to them, an abstract concept in the first place.

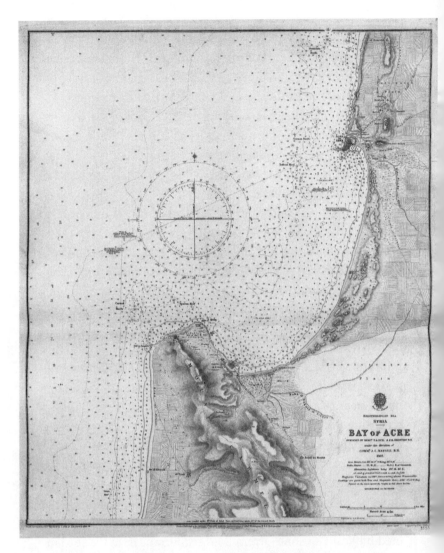

The Bay of Acre with the city of Acre in the center and Haifa on the promontory on the upper left. Engraved by J & C Walker, published by the British Admiralty, 1863. *Courtesy of the Eran Laor Collection, Hebrew University.*

But it didn't really matter what the Ottomans called the region or how they divided it. Palestine, land of many names—Zion, Eretz Israel, or even the Arabic Filistin— ignited the imaginations of nineteenth-century Americans like no other place on Earth. To them, it was sacred, filled with transcendent meanings. There were always two Palestines in one space: the landscape of the visible and the tangible, and, no less real, the landscape of faith and imagination. Americans in Palestine constantly attempted to find evidence of prophetic anticipation and fulfillment in the landscape, in effect reading the holy landscape as if it were a book.[23] Some American Protestants even called Palestine "the Fifth Gospel."[24] William Thomson, missionary in the Holy Land for thirty years, explained that

> In a word, Palestine is one vast table whereupon God's messages to men have been drawn, and graven deep in living characters by the Great Publisher of glad tidings, to be seen and read of all to the end of time. The Land and the Book—with reverence be it said—constitute the entire and all perfect text, and should be studied together.[25]

Lynch visited the grotto beneath the Carmelite Monastery where the monks believed Elijah had built his altar. Exemplifying Thomson's comment, he connected the land and the Bible by recalling verse from the King James Bible: "Then the fire of the Lord fell and consumed the burnt sacrifice, and the wood and the stones and the dust, and licked up the water that was in the trench."[26] Throughout his adventures in Palestine, like other Americans after him, Lynch continued to discover—sometimes with questionable accuracy—the exact location of events in the Bible, should he happen to traverse a promising location for, say, the place where Jacob wrestled with the angel or Christ preached the Sermon on the Mount.

While Lynch was ashore, waiting for the wind and surf to abate, the expedition's enlisted men gathered together aboard the *Supply*, away from the other seamen, and pondered what lay ahead for them. Like other enlisted men, they wore the traditional blue woolen uniform with white collar and cuffs. Regulations allowed them to have close-cropped beards if they chose, though longer, muttonchop whiskers could reach one inch below the ear as long as the chops aligned with the corners of the mouth.

Lynch had carefully selected the sailors for the expedition; all nine were American born, young, strong, and, Lynch believed, of sober disposition. Their names were: Charles Albertson, Charles Horner, Gilbert Lea, George Lockwood, Henry Loveland, George Overstock, Hugh Read, John Robinson, and Francis Williams. Each sailor had pledged to abstain from alcohol and tobacco for the duration of the expedition, vices that Lynch thought would distract them from the significance of their mission. Such a pledge was unusual, for enlisted men in navies of the period relished their "liberties" in port when released from strict ship discipline. Often, they spent all their accumulated wages in short periods of drunken debauchery.

These young men may have agreed to abstain from alcohol and tobacco; however, they hadn't pledged to abstain from gossip. A rumor was circulating about a curse on Dead Sea expeditions: Never was an expedition planned to explore the region of the Dead Sea which prospered. Previous expedition members were rumored to have died from illness; some were robbed and killed by the bloodthirsty Arabs, though no one knew specifics. However, after pondering the merits of the so-called curse, the sailors agreed that the other expeditions hadn't been American, and Yankees don't flinch. One said American sailors feared "neither the wandering Arab nor the withering influence of disease," and they consoled themselves that swords, pistols, revolvers, carbines, and a blunderbuss would protect them. Indeed, they seemed inordinately fond of the blunderbuss that, as one said, was "able to scatter some fatal doses" of buckshot.[27]

The Americans—like their predecessors, Costigan and Molyneux—were about to face heat, lack of sufficient fresh food and water, dangerous Bedouin tribes, and possible death far from home. The region was politically unstable, nominally governed by the Ottoman Empire, with real power in the hands of tribal chiefs. According to legend, no one could sail upon the Dead Sea and live. Outside the few towns, there would be no recourse for assistance.

They were on their own.

II

The Great Age of Exploration

The harbor at Hampton Roads in Norfolk, Virginia, was a magical place in the early nineteenth century, especially for a teenaged boy watching the great square-rigged sailing warships tack past Sewell's Point into the harbor, their sails shifting with the wind. The waterfront had been home to the country's first navy yard, which the British burned twice— during the Revolutionary War and the War of 1812. Years after Lynch's fateful expedition, the first battle between ironclad warships—the USS *Monitor* and the CSS *Virginia* (formerly the USS *Merrimack*)—would occur here, just off Sewell's Point.

It was a place of mystery to the uninitiated, with wooden ships of war hull to hull along the wharf, their long bowsprits jutting over walkways and streets. A forest of masts, spars,

and rigging rose from them. Dockworkers shouted to each other as they loaded and unloaded cargo. On ships readying for sea, fleet-footed sailors, dressed in wide-bottomed canvas trousers, ran up and down the ratlines—horizontal ropes used as steps on the masts—as comfortable as if they had been on level ground.

The nineteenth century was the grand age of sailing ships, even for America, a young nation newly liberated from Britain, the queen of the oceans. In the beginning, America faced the sea, founded as it was with a collection of villages, like Norfolk, strung along the coastline for easy access first for fishing and whaling, then for merchant voyages to the Old World, the Far East, and beyond.

Legend surrounded some of the warships frequenting Hampton Roads, such as four of six frigates commissioned by Congress in 1794 to begin the American navy that were still afloat: the *Constitution, United States, Congress,* and *Constellation.* All saw distinguished service during the War of 1812, battling ships such as the French frigate *L'Insurgente,* and the British HMS *Java,* HMS *Cyane,* and HMS *Belvidera.* In times of peace, both merchantmen and navy ships left for destinations that, for a young boy, would have seemed almost too exotic to exist—the West Indies, the Mediterranean, the East Indies, the China Sea, and the South Pacific.

As a young boy, Lynch felt the irrepressible tug of the sea and committed himself to it as a lifelong vocation. Years later, he wrote, "At the age of sixteen, with the love of adventure enkindled by the very perils arrayed to deter me, I abandoned my studies, and embraced the roving, stirring, homeless, comfortless, but attractive life of a sailor."[28]

In the pre-Annapolis navy, the only route to a career as a navy officer lay in a midshipman's billet on a ship of war, where a young man could learn the trade on the high seas. It wasn't easy work—even after the violent seasickness of the early voyage passed. Midshipmen studied mathematics and navigation during time off from standing watches any hour of day or night. They slept in hammocks of hemp cloth, wedged closely together, swaying with the motion of the ship, gentle or rough. Below deck was often stiflingly hot and smelled nauseatingly of bilge water. Food was bland and boring. For months on end, once the crew consumed the fresh food, their fare consisted mostly of hard tack (ships biscuits) complete with weevils, salt tack (meat preserved in salt), tea, and coffee. Each midshipman had a two-foot-square wooden locker for his belongings. During battle, the lockers were lashed together to form the surgeon's operating table. But even in peace, diseases such as yellow fever, malaria, cholera, and typhoid threatened a sailor's life.

In 1819, the legendary USS *Congress*, a thirty-six-gun frigate, was readying at Hampton Roads for an extensive cruise to the waters near the Philippines and China, the first American warship to do so. Lynch had obtained his papers as a midshipman, a difficult task because of the limited slots available in a peacetime navy. In May, the *Congress*, with Lynch aboard, sailed first to the Azores, then Rio de Janeiro and the Cape of Good Hope on its way to the China Sea. Its mission was to establish a protective presence against pirates for the many American merchantmen plying those distant Asian waters.[29] Over the next few years, Midshipman Lynch served on ships that patrolled the South China Sea and the coast of South America, fought pirates in the Caribbean, and reconnoitered the Mediterranean. His captains included some of the navy's leaders, such as

David Dixon Porter and Matthew C. Perry, who later forcibly opened trade with Japan.

One of the most influential of Lynch's early navy associations was the friendship he formed with Matthew Fontaine Maury, later the first director of the US Naval Observatory and a founder of modern oceanography. Midshipman Lynch met him while aboard the *Brandywine*, a new frigate named in honor of the battle in which the Marquis de Lafayette was wounded during the Revolutionary War. Under command of Captain Charles Morris, the frigate was rushed to completion in 1825 because President John Quincy Adams had decided that the ship would transport Lafayette back to France at the end of his year-long grand tour of America.

Maury, himself newly a midshipman, arrived for duty on the *Brandywine* clutching a new copy of Nathaniel Bowditch's *American Practical Navigator* and dressed in his just-purchased blue wool uniform. The *Brandywine*, in black paint with a yellow band along her gun ports, was riding at anchor in the Potomac River near Greenleaf's Point. Midshipman Lynch joined a few days later, just before Lafayette's arrival. The number of midshipmen had been increased to twenty-six from the usual eleven for a frigate, to give more young men the opportunity to journey with the revolutionary hero. However, that increase left the young men hardly room to stand in their quarters in steerage.[30]

In high winds on September 8, 1825, crewmen lined the yards and rigging when a commodore's launch approached the *Brandywine*. The midshipmen stood at attention in their dress uniforms—short jackets of blue wool with six brass buttons on each lapel, standing collars with gold lace braid on each side, and black cravats. All strained until they could see the sixty-eight-year-old Lafayette, accompanied by his son, George Washington Lafayette. The frigate's guns roared a seventeen-gun salute, and the crew swung Lafayette aboard in a specially constructed bosun's chair so that he wouldn't have to climb the side of the wildly rocking frigate. In the days to come, as they crossed the Atlantic to France, Lafayette spoke to the junior officers, including Lynch and Maury, with an attitude of "paternal friendship" as he told them stories about George Washington and the revolution.[31]

Maury and Lynch bonded over an interest in books. Their friendship continued even as they served on other ships and rose through the ranks. In 1842, Maury became the first superintendent of the Naval Observatory, and in that role he engaged ship captains in his oceanic research, using knowledge from that research to publish many navigational charts and influential books that revolutionized sailors' use of currents and wind. Discussions between the two surely added fuel to Lynch's desire to become an explorer.

In the first half of the nineteenth century, especially outside the well-known routes across the Atlantic and the Mediterranean, the world's oceans and seas were still mysterious places. Charts often were misleading, wrong, or nonexistent. So-called scientists of the day manufactured fantastic theories accepted as true until disproven.

One arcane theory that persisted well into the Victorian era involved the viscosity of water. Many believed that water pressure increased the density of water, so that objects falling into the ocean would sink until the density of the object matched the density of the water. A chest of gold coins, for example, would sink deeper than a damaged dinghy. Horses would sink lower than humans, and all these objects would hang suspended forever in the viscous layers of the ocean.

Matthew Fontaine Maury, Lynch's lifelong friend from their midshipman days, was the first superintendent of the Naval Observatory. *Courtesy of Wikimedia Commons.*

When discussion of transatlantic telegraph cables began in the 1850s, some critics hotly contested the idea of cable crossing a deep body of water, saying that the cables would not be heavy enough to sink to the ocean floor. The theory of the compressed density of water was not totally dispelled until Maury, then at the Naval Observatory, arranged to study samples of mud brought up from thousands of feet down. When he found sand, crushed shells, coral, and other lightweight items in the mud, it was obvious that such items would sink rather than remain suspended in mid-water layers.[32]

Another of these curious yet persistent theories concerned the North and South Poles. The Earth consisted of concentric, habitable spheres, claimed former army captain and self-appointed scientist John Symmes, who lectured widely in the mid-1820s. The poles, said Symmes, possessed holes large enough that sailing ships could voyage from the polar seas across into other spheres. Jeremiah Reynolds, a former newspaper editor, became enamored of Symmes's theory and promoted an American exploring expedition to test the idea of holes in the polar caps leading to other worlds. After Symmes died, Reynolds distanced himself from "Symmes's Holes" but continued to promote the idea of an exploring expedition.[33]

By 1828, Samuel Southard, secretary of the navy under John Quincy Adams, became interested in the exploring expedition concept, and Congress, with the backing of President Adams, approved funds for a major naval expedition. Both the British and French navies had sponsored major explorations in the past, such as Captain James Cook's expeditions (1768–79), but America hadn't mounted a major expedition since the 1803 Lewis and Clark Corps of

Discovery Expedition searched for the Northwest Passage. Why shouldn't the US Navy do something similar?

The neophyte nineteenth-century American Navy couldn't hope to match the exploits of the British Navy, more than twice its size. While Americans were debating the specifications of the expedition, the British dispatched HMS *Beagle* to the Pacific (1831–36) with budding naturalist Charles Darwin aboard. A few years later, Captain James Clark Ross sailed to the Antarctic with HMS *Erebus* and *Terror* (1839–43). John Franklin's first two expeditions (1819–22 and 1825–27) surveyed much of the Northwest American and Canadian coasts. His fatal 1845 expedition was lost in the frozen wilderness while attempting to chart the Northwest Passage. Counting them all, in the decades after Cook's voyages, Britain mounted twenty-eight expeditions and France seventeen. Even Holland, Spain, and Russia managed thirteen between them.

In 1838, the United States Exploring Expedition—often called the Ex Ex—set sail from Hampton Roads. While most European expeditions consisted of two or three ships, America mounted a squadron of six, an extraordinary effort for a country with such a small navy.

As befitting a squadron, the commander, Charles Wilkes, a slender man with brown hair, who appeared careworn and older than his forty-one years, wore a captain's uniform and flew a commodore's pennant. Peculiar factors were at play, though: Wilkes was only a lieutenant, not a captain, and was not entitled to the uniform or the pennant. Upon return of the expedition in 1842, Lieutenant Wilkes was court-martialed for killing some eighty inhabitants of Malolo Island in the South Pacific, exercising excessive force in punishing his men, falsifying the mapping of the Antarctic, and other grievances. The court of navy captains aboard the USS *North Carolina* in New York Harbor, after lengthy testimony, only reprimanded Wilkes. He was later court-martialed and suspended for publically criticizing Gideon Welles, secretary of the navy, in an editorial in the *New York Times*.

The expedition sounded good on paper: circumnavigation of the globe to seek out new lands, navigation routes, and commerce opportunities. Among the 346 men on board were two naturalists, two botanists, a mineralogist, and two artists. Even more obscure sciences were also represented: a conchologist (studying mollusks and shells) and a philologist. An accompanying taxidermist preserved specimens.

But expedition planners squabbled over priorities and performed much behind-the-scenes maneuvering from the start. Some eighteen months after Congress approved funding, the new secretary of the navy, Mahlon Dickerson, under President Andrew Jackson, decided that the objective of the expedition was to promote the interests of American merchant ships, whalers, and sealers by charting little known regions of the oceans and establishing an American presence there. Scientific research was "comparatively of secondary importance."[34] Dickerson procrastinated about expedition details to the degree that Captain Thomas ap Catesby Jones asked to be relieved as commander and Maury resigned as the official astronomer. The expedition didn't sail until ten years after funding approval.

Jones was replaced with Wilkes, an expert in scientific navigation who had journeyed to Europe to buy scientific equipment and solicit advice from scientific societies. However, captains of the other ships immediately complained about someone of lower rank and less experience at sea being put in charge. Still, the accomplishments of the expedition were impressive: Wilkes sailed without decent charts of the Antarctic or South Pacific. His careful survey-ing created 180 new charts of territory, including nearly a thousand miles of Antarctic coastline, some 280 islands in the Pacific, and much of what is now the West Coast of America (then belonging to Spain or American land con-tested with Britain).[35]

The expedition's scientists collected thousands of arti-facts and specimens, including 150 mammals, 2,000 birds, 50,000 plants, 1,000 corals, crustaceans, and mollusks, as well as more than 5,000 human artifacts. At first, Joseph Henry, head of the Smithsonian, refused to house the haul, perhaps not realizing its value or perhaps because of the lingering controversy surrounding the expedition. Henry eventually agreed to accept, provided that the specimens and artifacts were stored somewhere else. Today, the collections from the Ex Ex form an invaluable part of the institution's core collections.[36]

In the 1830s and early 1840s, the conservative and budget-strapped American Navy, led by men who had acquired all their knowledge of the sea in sailing ships, saw no reason to modernize. However, a number of policies of the peacetime navy disturbed young officers, including Lynch and Maury. They criticized the uneven training that resulted from the lack of a naval academy similar to the US Army's academy at West Point and the lag in response of the navy to changes in technology.

Exhibiting an impulsiveness that did not serve his best interests, Lynch, in 1840, approached Secretary of the Navy James Paulding personally, without obeying the chain of command—a clear breach of protocol. Lynch urged a number of reforms, including the founding of a naval academy. After listening to what he had to say, Paulding ordered Lynch to leave Washington at once. Not long after, though, Paulding suggested a bill to Congress that contained many of Lynch's ideas. Congress established the US Naval Academy five years later under Secretary of the Navy George Bancroft.

The situation began to change, however, in 1841. Abel Upshur, secretary of the navy under President Tyler, committed to a navy strong enough to protect American commerce, saying, "Wars often arise from a rivalry in trade, and from the conflicts of interests which belong to it." A powerful navy prevented disputes from becoming war, he believed, and America needed a navy at least half the size of the British Navy. Upshur launched a home squadron, reasoning that if ships were all on distant stations, it would take too long to recall them in time of attack.[37]

In the mid-1840s, the navy's commercial role expanded along with increased trade abroad and in concert with the prevailing sentiments of Manifest Destiny, the idea that America was predestined to extend from the Atlantic to the Pacific. It may be easy to forget that, even after Texas joined the Union in 1845, America didn't reach the Pacific officially until the Oregon Treaty with Britain in 1846.

But even Manifest Destiny wasn't a new idea. George Washington himself, as early as 1783, called the United States a "rising empire." He, Benjamin Franklin, and their contemporaries had in mind an *imperium*, a state that would continue to grow in territory and population as well as power. They believed America was heir apparent to Britain's empire in the New World.[38]

Whether in government or the armed forces, expansionists weren't happy that California belonged to Spain or, later, to Mexico. In 1841, Thomas ap Catesby Jones, the commodore of the navy's Pacific squadron, occupied Monterey on the California coast. He had received intelligence that a British squadron recently left the port of Callao in Peru, destination unknown (true), and that America was at war with Mexico (false). The boundary dispute between the United States and Britain over Oregon Territory hadn't yet been resolved, and he didn't want to chance the British claiming California as well. Two days later, when Jones realized his error, he apologized and withdrew from Monterey. Amazingly, the residents were sympathetic to his mistake, saying his reasoning was understandable.[39]

President James Polk also wanted California. In a draft of a letter that Secretary of State James Buchanan wrote to American ambassadors on May 11, 1846, the day America declared war on Mexico over a skirmish with Mexican troops at Matamoros, Buchanan declared that the United States had no intention of acquiring either California or New Mexico. Polk had Buchanan delete the reference to California, meaning he would not commit to disinterest in acquiring California. The Mexican-American War resulted in a land grab of massive proportions—parts of Mexican territory that eventually became the states of Texas, New Mexico, California, Nevada, Arizona, and part of Colorado.

After the Mexican-American War, the popularity of Manifest Destiny only increased. The belief in America's destiny of expansion developed a corollary—a gospel of commerce—that created both pressures on and opportunities for the American Navy. Indeed, it wasn't at all clear in 1848, after the war, that the limits of the American Empire were the Pacific Ocean and the Rio Grande. Some proponents of Manifest Destiny encouraged the idea of a continental empire for the United States that encompassed the whole

North American continent, if not both North and South America, despite a lack of interest on the part of Canadians or Mexicans. Such a powerful empire would also, by implication, expand in the Pacific, the Caribbean, and Asia.[40] Manifest Destiny was global, not continental.

The years between the Mexican-American War and the Civil War were heady days. From 1848 to 1860, the United States was not legally at war, but some citizens engaged in private skirmishes in the name of the nation, a practice that acquired the name "filibustering." Flouting international law and the US Neutrality Act of 1794, Americans often engaged in two or more filibustering expeditions at any one time. Cuba was a popular target, as was Nicaragua.[41]

Though profit motivated some, many filibusters derived from a belief that conquered territories would benefit from the American way of life—its government, religion, and culture. The roots of this belief date from the Puritan vision of America as a "city upon a hill." Americans, believing themselves blessedly well intentioned, wanted to share their utopia with less fortunate peoples. For them, the prospect of a global empire in no way conflicted with the principles of the Revolutionary War. Rejecting British imperialism did not mean rejecting imperialism altogether. They believed territorial expansion was natural and inevitable.[42]

Most Americans of the antebellum years, though, supported a more restrained vision of Manifest Destiny, rejecting further expansion through war. They were after commerce and religious converts, not colonies. Americans believed in liberty—that the country use its emerging power not to oppress free peoples but to free oppressed ones. They believed in the proliferation of the American way of life through investment in foreign commerce, missionary zeal, and other "peaceful" means. Actual annexation of new ter-ritories outside the continent was not necessary—at least not in the antebellum period.[43]

America's 1848 mission to Palestine, though it seems curious today, grew naturally from its place in time—a world with blank spaces on maps ready for exploration and an expansionist country convinced of the superiority of its way of life. But there wouldn't have been an 1848 expedi-tion to the Dead Sea without Lynch. It is impossible to know exactly what caused him to propose the mission. He had long desired to visit the Holy Land. Then he learned of other countries' expeditions that tried and failed to establish that the Dead Sea was below sea level, which probably gave him the idea. But it was more than just a desire to compete with Europe's scientists and explorers that motivated him. Showing that the Dead Sea, in its ravaged landscape, was unique in this way would "prove" his fire and brimstone version of Protestantism. Then add his fervent American ethnocentrism, his desire to proselytize the American way of life, and his hero's bravura, and his complex motivation may become clearer. But whatever his reasons, he was about to put his life and others' lives in mortal danger.

III

Challenges Ashore

Finally, the wind shifted and moderated as the storm passed. The smooth sea allowed the other officers and the seamen to land the expedition's supplies and equipment from the *Supply* onto the beach near Haifa where Lynch waited. In addition to armaments, the inventory included canvas tents, water bags, gum-elastic bags for use as life preservers, cooking utensils, provisions, books, and a medicine chest. In the unlikely event of rain, each man received an India-rubber cap, leggings, and a coat; for sleeping, a piece of India-rubber cloth on which to lie and a blanket for cover.

Lynch had obtained some of the finest scientific instruments available, knowing from long experience how essential it was to have functioning tools when lives—and the expedition's mission—depended upon them. His level and theodolite came from London manufacturers Troughton and Simms, and his sextants were expensive precision instruments from the Paris shop of Henri-Prudence Gambey, the same manufacturer who supplied the United States Exploring Expedition. The yard-long, fragile mountain barometers with siphon tubes were also French, made by Bunten. His two English chronometers had been delayed but caught up with the expedition in Beirut. Only the weighted heaving line for measuring water depth was American, fashioned with a newly designed sampling cup at the end, used to test the composition of ocean or lake bottom samples.[44]

As arranged from Beirut, Lynch sent a message to the Ottoman governor at Acre asking for horses to be delivered both to ride and to pull the boats on their custom-made wheeled carriages. Near the water, but just outside the walls of Haifa, the crew pitched camp for the first night. Bordering the site were a graveyard and a dry well in what could have been a grotto but for the lack of moisture. A nearby carob tree resembled an apple tree, though it bore bitter beans instead of sweet fruit. The two tents—one for the officers, the other for the crew—were round rather than the more common rectangle so that the boats' masts could stand as center support poles.

The unmasted metal boats floated nearby, both flying the American flag. The men hoisted another American flag over the camp. One of the boats, built of copper, they named the *Fanny Mason*, after the young daughter of the secretary of the navy, and the other, constructed of iron, the *Fanny Skinner*, after the daughter of a senior commodore. One of the men, writing in his journal, thought the tranquil scene worthy of an artist's sketch.[45] The local population—wearing colorful,

From Beirut, the expedition brought Mustafa, the cook, along with an Arabic-speaking dragoman who served as a translator.

flowing clothes the Americans thought picturesque, though dirty—was so intrigued by the appearance of the American camp that a crowd gathered. Believing them to be gold, some of the crowd stole the small copper chains of the boat oarlocks.

The sailors assembled the carriages that would transport the two metal boats. The cook, Mustafa, whom they brought from Beirut along with an Arabic-speaking dragoman, prepared tea, their first refreshment in Palestine. When night came, sentries were posted as befitted a military camp. According to Lynch, "The stars were exceedingly brilliant; the air clear and cool—almost too cool,—and the surf beat in melancholy cadence, interrupted only by the distant cry of jackals in the mountains." He couldn't resist adding that the jackals were probably the same kind of foxes whose tails the biblical Samson tied together.[46]

One of the men started singing "Carry Me Back to Ole Virginny," and the others pounced on him for wishing to be home before the adventure had begun. The sailors didn't want to go home, not yet, not until, as one said, "They've been t' bottom o' the Dead Sea, and seen the spires and churches, and wine stores of old Sodom and Gomorrah."[47]

"For the first time outside the consulate, perhaps," Lynch noted, "the American flag has been raised in Palestine. May it be the harbinger of renewal to a now hapless people!"[48] Like the Puritans coming to America, he cast his covetous eye on the landscape but framed his designs in a scriptural light. The resilience of conflating America with the Holy Land came not from a desire to imitate the past but from an aspiration to bring the sacred past forward into the present. They would come, like the Puritans, "not to usurp but to claim, not to displace an alien culture but to repossess what was already theirs by promise."[49]

Any foray into Muslim lands, though, inevitably invoked memories of the two wars with the Barbary States, those thorns in America's side that threatened its commerce and besmirched its pride for thirty years. In those years, Barbary pirates captured thirty-five American ships and imprisoned for ransom some seven hundred men.[50] Ending the Barbary threat required two wars and much contentious national debate about the only two alternatives, neither attractive to the fledgling nation: They could pay tribute and ransoms—anathema to freedom-loving Americans—or they had to finance a large and permanent navy, also abhorrent to a newly self-determined people who only reluctantly agreed on a strong central government. It took those thirty full years of indecision between tribute or warfare—while doing some of both—before public opinion and government initiative solidified behind fielding a navy that could subdue the Barbary States, free the captives, and protect American shipping in the Mediterranean.

Americans still remembered how, in 1815, a US squadron, under the command of Captain Stephen Decatur, defeated the *Mashuda*, the Algerian flagship, taking four hundred of her crew prisoner. The Americans then surprised Omar Pasha, the new bey of Algiers, by appearing in his harbor with ten warships, an unprecedented show of strength. Not wanting to accept that he couldn't defeat the enhanced American fleet, the bey appealed to the British, citing their assurance during the War of 1812 "that the Americans would be swept from the seas in six months." Now the Americans were employing some of Britain's captured ships to threaten him, he protested. The tides of war had changed, however, and Britain could no longer help him against the upstart United States.[51]

Captain Decatur and William Shaler, the new US consul, famously offered treaty terms "dictated at the mouths of our cannon."[52] Shaler for his part didn't shy from stating his opinion of the people of Algiers and their religion: "Islamism, which requires little instruction . . . seems peculiarly adapted to the conceptions of barbarous people." It amazed him that so "worthless a power, should have been so long permitted to vex the commercial world and extort ransom."[53]

Forcing the Barbary States to agree to terms lifted America's stature as a nation both abroad and at home. "The name of an American is now the proudest in the world," bragged the widely read *Niles' Weekly Register*.[54] "We are greatly mistaken if this war with Algiers does not give it additional influence in the councils of Europe."

The bey had forsworn attacking American ships—but not those of other countries. A year after the Decatur attack, a combined Anglo-Dutch squadron attacked Algiers. As one British historian wrote, "It was not to be endured that England should tolerate what America had resented and punished."[55]

American flags and images of the bald eagle multiplied amid the renewed sense of national identity. The Barbary Wars forever changed Americans' perception of their own country, instilling a sense of pride in the neophyte nation, summarized by Decatur's famous phrase, "My country, right or wrong."[56]

Saturday, April 1—Just past midnight, the horses arrived, accompanied by the tinkling of bells. The argument between the dragoman and the leader of the muleteers woke anyone who might be sleeping, though the sailors couldn't understand the foreign tongue.

At first light, though, they saw the problem. The horses, which Lynch had procured sight unseen, were skinny and worn out. One seaman bemoaned that they were like the "butcher's market horses at home."[57] Still, they were horses—and essential to haul the boats. The men harnessed them to the carriages bearing the metal boats with the anticipation that the party would be able to travel without delay.

Then a crucial and unexpected flaw developed that threatened the whole enterprise: The horses wouldn't pull. They had been broken to saddle, not to haul loads under harness. The more the sailors urged the horses, the more they reared and kicked. The men found four horses that would pull, two to each carriage, but the load of metal boats and supplies proved too much for them. The men didn't expect the local horses to heave like the ones at home, but they did expect some movement, something between stock-still and a gallop. After all, they used horses for hauling in Palestine—didn't they?

Neither coaxing nor flogging worked; nor did removing the expedition's supplies a few items at a time until they had lightened the load down to just the boats. At one point, the horses moved forward a few feet, and the men rejoiced, thinking they had found an arrangement that would work. But then the horses backed unstoppably—no matter what the men tried—until the boats, still lashed to the carriages, slid into the water. Lashed as they were to the carriages, the boats didn't float. Rather, they started to disappear beneath the water. The men gave up, unlashed the boats from the carriages, and relaunched them in the bay.

Lynch had planned to head inland from Haifa across the hills to the Sea of Galilee, but now the deficiencies of the horses forced him to detour to Acre, the ancient seat of government across the bay. He would have to lodge a protest in person with Sa'id Bey, governor of Acre, who had procured the animals, and he would have to negotiate with the Ottoman bureaucracy, which he had hoped to avoid by landing at Haifa instead of Acre in the first place.

Palestine might be a backwater of the Ottoman Empire, but an armed expedition traversing its landscape still required the permission of Sultan Abdul Mejid. As such, the *Supply* had stopped briefly for Lynch to have an audience with the sultan in Istanbul—or Constantinople, as Americans insisted upon calling it.

The Ottoman Empire fascinated Americans, conjuring images of minarets, camels, exotic dancers, palm trees, and sand dunes. It recalled half-forgotten stories of savage violence with which the empire, rising up from territories to the south of what still was Constantinople then, had conquered and absorbed cultures stretching from the Persian Gulf to western North Africa within a few centuries.

The ferocious Ottoman army had threatened to overrun Christian Europe, stopped only by the 1683 defeat at the Battle of Vienna. The terror and devastation of that invasion lingered in the collective memory of Europe, even as the "Ottoman peril" waned, remaining an image of dark, demonic hordes that could arise at any moment to threaten Christian civilization.[58] They had come out of the desert to outstrip Rome. Someday, might a spark reignite that passion? After all, the empire had existed "uneasily close" to Christian Europe, not only geographically but culturally. Islam seemed to many a distorted mirror's reflection of borrowed and modified Judeo-Christian traditions. Even worse, the Ottoman Empire ruled biblical lands not with reverence and respect but with indifference and neglect. All these fears, hostilities, and fascinations lingered in the nineteenth-century American imagination—and fueled it.

So it was in 1800, with some trepidation that Captain William Bainbridge in the USS *George Washington* entered the narrow and heavily fortified Dardanelles on the way to Constantinople. The frigate was carrying half a million dollars' worth of trade goods that the United States had sent that year to Algiers as tribute. The Algerian ruler had ignominiously ordered Captain Bainbridge to transport the American tribute, supplemented by millions more from Algiers to the Ottoman sultan as Algiers's annual tribute to their overlord. Bainbridge lacked a *firman*, an imperial decree guaranteeing safe passage, and was unable to traverse the narrow strait without entering range of the fort's guns, so he risked a clever ruse. Bainbridge fired an eight-gun salute to the fort. The fort fired a salute in return. Instead of waiting to be boarded for a check of credentials, as expected, Bainbridge made full sail out of range before the fort's weapons could reload.

The Ottoman capital known for being especially friendly to Westerners, but this time, perhaps influenced by the millions that the American ship carried, Bainbridge and his officers received a warm welcome. The Ottomans admired that America—which they thought an island kingdom—had successfully rebelled from European rule. Moreover, the Americans had not exhibited any imperialist craving for Ottoman lands. European countries, in contrast, circled like vultures waiting for weaknesses—particularly Russia, which desired the empire's warm-water ports.[59]

Before Bainbridge departed, he obtained a reprieve for the commander of the Dardanelles fort, whom the sultan had not only relieved of his command but whom he had summarily condemned to death for allowing the Americans to trick him into letting the ship pass unmolested.[60]

Almost a half century later, Lynch arrived at the Cherighan Palace for his own interview with the Sultan Abdul Mejid to obtain a firman for the expedition to traverse Palestine, descend the Jordan River, and explore the Dead Sea. Accompanied by an interpreter from the American legation, he entered a room with a magnificent view of the Bosporus. Sheffie Bey, the sultan's confidential secretary, offered him a "chibouque [water pipe], the bowl of which

Sultan Abdul Mejid, ruler of the Ottoman Empire, which loosely controlled Palestine in 1848. Lynch aroused controversy when he refused to relinquish his officer's sword before his audience with the sultan in Istanbul to obtain permission for the expedition to explore the Jordan River and the Dead Sea. The sultan granted the request anyway. *Courtesy of the Library of Congress.*

was eight feet distant, with a jasmine stem between, having a mouthpiece of the purest and costliest amber, encircled with diamonds." Lynch wasn't a smoker, but he joked in his memoir of the voyage, "As an opportunity of inhaling the odour of the weed of royalty might never again present itself, my inclinations jumped accordant with the rules of etiquette, and I puffed away with as much vivacity as any Turk."[61]

Lynch, like other visitors, described the court as magnificent:

> It is oblong, and contains about four acres, laid out in parterres and gravel walks, with many young and thrifty trees, and a great variety of plants: flowers there were few, for it was yet early in the season. In the centre, with a graveled walk between, were two quadrangular, artificial ponds, in which a number of gold and silver fish were gamboling in security, protected as they were from the talons of the cormorant by nets drawn over a few feet above the surface of the water. The fish sporting beneath, the bird of prey poised above, ready for a swoop through the first rent of the flimsy screen, seemed fitting emblems of the feeble Turk and the vigorous and grasping Russian.[62]

Lynch was led to the southern wing of the palace and ascended to a landing and to the door of the throne room. Then the American captain created a stir. He refused to give up his sword, as required before entering the sultan's presence. He told the chamberlain that the audience was given to him as an officer of the United States. The sword was part of his uniform as an officer, and he could not dispense with it. If denied an audience because he would not remove his sword, there would be no firman, and without the firman, no landing in Palestine. Still, Lynch had decided: no sword, no audience.

Lynch described the sultan as "a man, young in years, but evidently of impaired and delicate constitution, his wearied and spiritless air was unrelieved by any indication of intellectual energy."[63] Lynch presented him with "some biographies and prints, illustrative of the character and habits of our North American Indians, the work of American artists" and obtained the firman that he needed. Considering their two positions—one an upstart ambitious adventurer, the other a dynastic ruler held captive by centuries of tradition in a gilded cage—Lynch reflected:

> *While in his presence, I could not refrain from drawing comparisons and moralizing on fate. There was the Sultan, an Eastern despot, the ruler of mighty kingdoms and the arbiter of the fate of millions of his fellow-creatures; and, face to face, a few feet distant, one, in rank and condition, among the very humblest servants of a far-distant republic; and yet, little as life has to cheer, I would not change positions with him, unless I could carry with me my faith, my friendships, and my aspirations. My feelings saddened as I looked upon the monarch, and I thought of Montezuma.*[64]

His description may sound condescending, but he had good cause.

Notorious for governmental corruption and inefficiency, the Ottoman Empire had fallen upon hard times. Despite recent attempts to reform and modernize, the industrial revolution had largely bypassed the empire. Its farming methods were antiquated, and there were few modern roads even in major cities. In 1808, Muhammad Ali seized control of Egypt. Though he called himself viceroy, Ali paid little attention to the sultan and, at times, was more or less at war with him. The viceroy's adopted son, Ibrahim Pasha, conquered Palestine and Syria, and it required the combined British, French, and Austrian forces to drive Ibrahim Pasha back into Egypt.

The European powers strategically returned control of the region to the Ottomans, a weaker and less threatening government than the Egyptian regime. The Greeks, too, broke from the empire in 1821 and achieved independence after ten years of bloody rebellion. Through treaties in 1829 and 1833, Russia, concomitantly growing in power as the Ottoman Empire diminished, gained influence with the empire that caused European powers to worry about their overland access to India and the Far East.

American John Lloyd Stephens wrote in 1839 of the empire "which once sent forth large and terrible armies, burning, slaying, and destroying, shaking the hearts of princes and peoples, now like a fallen giant, huge, unwieldy, and helpless, ready to fall into the hands of the first invader, and dragging out a precarious and ignoble existence but by the mercy of the great Christian powers."[65]

The Ottoman Empire might be dying, but it was still capable of vicious acts, of which Lynch was well aware. When the *Supply* sought refuge from a storm near Scio (Chios) on the way to Beirut, Lynch saw the ruins from the 1822 Chios Massacre, when the Ottomans destroyed the island's villages to quell a Greek separatist movement. Estimates of residents killed run from an appalling "conservative" figure of twenty-five thousand dead and forty-five thousand sold into slavery to an even more frightening high

The Massacre at Chios by Eugène Delacroix (1824). When the *Supply* stopped at Chios to wait out a storm, Lynch visited the ruins left after the massacre. *Courtesy of De l'histoire de l'art.*

of eighty thousand to ninety thousand killed.[66] "On landing, we found ourselves amid a scene of desolation," Lynch said, "an entire city, with all its environs, laid in ruins by the ruthless Turks during that darkest hour of Turkish history, the massacre of Scio. . . . Nearly every house was unroofed and in ruins."[67] Destructive power still coursed through the old empire's veins.

Lynch had orders from the secretary of the navy to obtain the firman, but he also had no illusions about the degree of protection that a firman would convey upon his expedition. "It could afford none whatever; for Eastern travelers well know that, ten miles east of a line drawn from Jerusalem to Nabulus, the tribes roam uncontrolled, and rob and murder with impunity."[68]

A firman's power derived more from its absence than its presence. If Lynch had not obtained one, he would have no claim on any help or protection from Ottoman officials. But with the firman in hand, he could send word from Beirut asking the governor of Acre to obtain horses for the expedition. The inferior creatures presented in the middle of the night showcased the attitude of an Ottoman official out of range of the sultan's wrath. He complied—but not with any great enthusiasm, loyalty, or fear. With the firman, Lynch could ride safely around the bay from Haifa to Acre to protest the inferior condition of the animals, but he had no reason for optimism about what his protest might achieve.

A few of the men were detailed to sail the boats across the bay. The horses, pulling light loads of supplies in the carriages and encouraged with frequent applications of cudgels, were driven along the beach road to rejoin the boats at Acre. However, Lynch had not yet found a real solution to the problem, and this turn of events at the expedition's outset concerned and frustrated him. He had timed the expedition's arrival in Palestine for spring when floodwaters of the Jordan River would carry the boats over the rapids. A delay could result in increased danger during the navigation of the river. It could also expose the expedition to the intense summer heat that had caused the failure of the two previous expeditions to the Dead Sea and the deaths of their commanders.

An ancient port in what is now northern Israel, Acre has been inhabited at least since the time of Pharaoh Thutmose III (sixteenth century BC). In ancient times, the city served as a major center of commerce along the lines of Alexandria and Constantinople. But due to the gradual silting of the harbor and decline in the region's commerce, Acre had lost its international importance, though it was still a defensible walled city into the 1800s. Napoleon heavily damaged it with bombardments in 1799, as did Ibrahim Pasha in 1831, while capturing the city on his way to conquer Syria. In 1840, the combined British, French, and Austrian squadrons, as part of their campaign to defeat Ibrahim Pasha and restore Ottoman rule, reduced much of what remained of Acre to rubble.

Lynch rode there to seek Gabriel Nasralla, the American consul. Once he reached the town, he twisted and turned through narrow, labyrinthine streets, alleys, and bazaars. Shops displayed their wild profusion of spices in open containers: coriander, cumin, fennel, saffron, sumac, thyme, turmeric, and more. As he rode, Lynch caught sight of the American flag flying above the turret of the consul's house. He dismounted at the blank wall of a cul-de-sac and climbed a stone stairway. Crossing the remains of buildings destroyed in one of the bombardments, he finally reached the consul's house, which still had several cannon shot lodged in the walls. Lynch sat on a divan for the ritual coffee offered to guests and a briefing on the situation in Palestine.[69]

When he explored the terrace of the consul's house, Lynch could see down into the town and viewed women with golden hair-ornaments and ragged trousers. He spied, on another nearby terrace, "a young girl with a glorious pro-fusion of curling tresses, which fell from beneath a golden net-work on her head." He noted that her bodice, short pel-licle, and trousers were rather the worse for wear, but he would have admired "the dark, wild-looking eye and the luxuriant hair"—had Nasralla not told him that earlier the beautiful head had been observed going through an exami-nation for lice.[70] Lynch wasn't immune to the exotic appeal of the women in the Orient, though the erotic appeal of the exotic for him, as with many Western men, mixed with con-demnation as inferior and unclean.

Accompanied by Consul Nasralla, Lynch sought Sa'id Bey, the governor of Acre who administered the counties of Acre, Haifa, Safed, Nazareth, and Tiberias, all part of the province-district of Beirut.[71] The two located the governor chatting with a group of men in a cafe just outside the gate of the town. The governor's informal manner contrasted oddly with the richness of his gem-studded ring and the diamond-encircled amber mouthpiece of his long-stemmed pipe. Bey, Egyptian by descent and Syrian by upbringing, whose com-plexion Lynch described as mulatto, was about forty-five, with a black beard, and dressed in plain blue pantaloons, a long blue frock coat, and a red fez.

Lynch's firman endorsing the expedition required the governor—at least theoretically—to be helpful to the expe-dition. Indeed, one problem with previous expeditions by other countries was the failure to secure the appropriate firman from the Egyptian-controlled government in the 1830s. Sultan Abdel Mejid had been more accommodating.

Nasralla introduced Lynch to Bey, and they exchanged a few pleasantries. Then Lynch, ignoring the Muslim tradition of slow-paced negotiations—and probably the consul's advice—told Bey in direct American fashion that the horses he had provided were worthless.[72] The unflappable governor replied that he was deeply sorry, for "there were none better to be procured." Lynch proposed oxen, but Bey protested. "It was then the height of seed-time." He couldn't take the oxen from the fields without great injury to the farmers.[73]

Lynch found the governor's manner cunning, if not treacherous, for there were surely better horses in Palestine available for a price. He concluded that Bey wanted a bribe, which, though not unusual in the region, was abhorrent to the American. Lynch decided to disappoint Bey and, instead of offering a bribe, tried emphasizing the wider significance of the expedition. "We are not common travelers, but sent by a great country and with the sanction of your own government." Bey was unresponsive to that appeal, so Lynch tried emphasizing the sultan's firman. "Provide us with the means of transportation, for which we will pay liberally, but not extravagantly. Your own sovereign has expressed an interest in our labors, and if we are not assisted, I will take good care that the odium of failure should rest upon the shoulders of Sa'id Bey, governor of Acre."[74]

The threat didn't impress Bey either. Both men knew that Lynch's firman had limited value in Palestine, only loosely under the sultan's control. After meeting with the sultan in Constantinople to obtain the firman, Lynch had become pessimistic about Ottoman leadership because of the sultan's weary and spiritless manner. Lynch knew that Ottoman rule was in decline and, like many Americans, attributed this to the influence of the Muslim religion. Governor Bey's actions confirmed Lynch's worst opinion of Ottoman governance.[75]

Later that afternoon, Lynch responded to an invitation from Sa'id Bey to come to the palace, apparently for further negotiations. After traversing more of the twisting streets, stairs, and courtyards, he arrived at a room in the governor's home that was simply furnished with divans and crowded with officers in Ottoman uniforms. Bey, in contrast to Lynch, observed the niceties of politeness to guests, sincere or not, and invited Lynch to take the corner seat on the divan, the place of honor. Lynch was offered the traditional water pipe and coffee. On his right sat a judge, an older man in a cashmere robe with fur trimming, and next to the judge was the governor.

Lynch's attention drew to a Bedouin seated on the opposite leg of the L-shaped divan, whom he described as "a magnificent savage, enveloped in a scarlet cloth pelisse [cloak], richly embroidered with gold." The man had a rich olive complexion and glossy black hair. He radiated a suppressed violence as his hand played absently with the hilt of his curved sword. An Egyptian of the Hanabi tribe, he had come to Palestine as one of Ibrahim Pasha's men during the Egyptian occupation in 1831. By the time the British forced the Egyptian Army to retreat in 1840, the man had transformed himself into a local Bedouin chieftain and established a power base there.[76]

When Lynch settled on the divan with his coffee and the room became quiet, the governor stated alarming intelligence: "The tribes in the Ghor [Jordan River Valley] are up in arms, at war among themselves, and pillaging and maltreating all who fall into their hands." He pointed to the chieftain as the report's source, naming him, "'Akil Aga el Hasseé, a great border sheikh of the Arabs."[77] The governor proposed that the American expedition could not proceed safely without a hundred soldiers as guards and offered to provide the guards for twenty thousand piastres (about eight hundred dollars then). Bey didn't look at Lynch when he made the suggestion that the Americans should pay this outrageous sum for protection.

Lynch concluded that the sheikh was brought in to intimidate him and politely balked. A lengthy discussion ended with Lynch saying, "I am not authorized to accept such an offer. Even if I were authorized, I would scorn to buy protection. If draught horses can be procured or oxen furnished, I will pay fairly for them and for a few soldiers to act as scouts. We are well armed and able to protect ourselves."

The Bedouin of the Ghor "will eat you up," the sheikh suggested, a glint of amusement in his words.

The Bedouin would "find Americans difficult of digestion," Lynch replied steadfastly.[78]

Carefully scrutinizing the nonverbal cues in the room and feeling the ebb and flow of tension between the men, Lynch realized that the sheikh was playing along with the governor's game but was acting, in reality, as an independent agent. He trusted the sheikh more than the treacherous governor—or perhaps he thought it a good idea to make a friend of a potential adversary on the coming journey.

After they left the palace, Lynch caught up with the sheikh and asked him a few questions about the Bedouin of the Ghor. During their conversation, Lynch allowed the chieftain to examine his sword that had pistol barrels fastened near its hilt. The sheikh remarked that this combination of sword and pistol was "the devil's invention."

AKĪL AGA.

A Bedouin of the Hanabi tribe, Sheikh 'Akil Aga el Hasseé by 1843 had become chief of a group of irregulars in Northern Palestine. By 1847, he controlled Galilee from Haifa and Acre in the west to Tiberias in the east, with Nazareth in the center. His power expanded in the years to come.

Lynch informed the sheikh that his expedition had several of the sword-and-revolver combinations, as well as bowie-knife pistols, carbines, and a blunderbuss.

Impressed with the firepower, the sheikh agreed that the Americans might survive the dangerous Ghor. "You will if anyone can," he said.[79]

Lynch later learned of the sheikh's importance from Consul Nasralla: The previous year, the sheikh had led several tribes in rebellion against the Ottoman government, and, because they could not defeat him, the Ottomans bought him off by naming him a colonel.

While in Gibraltar, Lynch had received word of Bedouin attacks against the Molyneux expedition on its way down the Jordan. Moreover, after the exchange with the sheikh, Lynch confirmed the current danger of marauding Bedouin in the unsettled countryside with two other Americans who happened to be in Acre—a Major Smith of the US Engineers Corps and a Mr. Sergeants of New York, who had just traveled from Nazareth. Bedouin had attacked their group two nights before at the foot of Mount Tabor, near the route Lynch planned to take. The danger was real.

However, Lynch recoiled at the thought of bribing the governor for protection. Even if he had the money for such a purpose—which he hadn't—the thought of retreat proved even more repugnant. He wouldn't hesitate to risk his own life, but he was in a quandary about putting his men in danger. Like other military men of his era, Lynch looked upon his men not as individuals who might themselves agonize over danger, for only officers engaged in that kind of introspection. Rather like children, his men had to be protected for their own good and for the good of the mission. After mulling the problem, Lynch decided that he could gain the Bedouins' goodwill more likely by leading his party into their territory without an escort than if protected by an armed Ottoman force.

Thus, he petitioned the governor for ten men to act as scouts. When Sa'id Bey hesitated, Lynch withdrew the request and then refused the men when the governor tried to urge them upon him. Lynch realized that the governor might have been in collusion with previous attacks upon Americans, and it was better not to have Bey's men in his camp.

A wily strategist—despite an unwillingness to play the game of slow-paced, give-and-take negotiation involving accustomed bribes—Lynch preferred to solicit the aid not of the governor but of Sheikh 'Akil and of another whom he happened to meet at the governor's palace: Sharif Hazzâ of Mecca, a small man of about fifty years with a dark complexion, whom Lynch described as an Arab nobleman. The sharif was said to be a thirty-third lineal descendant of the Prophet and was the son and brother of the governors of Mecca until Muhammad Ali of Egypt had deposed them. Everyone treated Sharif Hazzâ with utmost respect.

When Lynch proposed that the sharif accompany them on the expedition, the older man smiled as if the proposition were absurd. He became interested, though, when Lynch explained to him that, instead of a party of private individuals, the expedition was made up of commissioned officers and seamen sent to solve a scientific question. Knowing that Muslims revered Moses as a Hebrew prophet, Lynch suggested that Moses's dire warnings in Deuteronomy about the sins of Sodom and Gomorrah incurring the wrath of God could be proven by an expedition to the Dead Sea. If the Dead Sea did indeed lie below sea level and the landscape showed evidence of the "brimstone, and salt, *and* burning," as claimed in Deuteronomy, that would prove that the region had been affected by a cataclysm of biblical proportions. Lynch said to the sharif that it would "convince the incredulous that Moses was a true prophet."[80]

After pondering Lynch's words, Sharif Hazzâ agreed to accompany the Americans, leaving the issue of payment for his services to Lynch's discretion. Hazzâ even offered to inquire if Sheikh 'Akil would be interested in joining the expedition. Pleased, Lynch wondered if Sharif Hazzâ had been providentially placed in his path for the benefit of the mission.

If Sharif Hazzâ was who Lynch believed him to be, he was a Hashemite, a member of the royal family historically entrusted with the protection of Mecca. To have a Hashemite accompanying the expedition was a true distinction. With Hazzâ and 'Akil joining them, the expedition would be less likely to be a target of marauding Bedouin tribes.

Before he even left the Mediterranean, Lynch had improved his expedition in two key ways over the deadly Costigan and Molyneux expeditions: First, the trip would take place in late spring rather than summer. Second, Lynch had made allies of an influential Bedouin chief and a member of the Hashemite royal family, whose presence would deter attacks.

Lynch told Sharif Hazzâ the truth, if not the whole truth, about his mission. He didn't explain that five other expeditions of British and European scientists since 1837 had attempted to demonstrate that the Dead Sea lay below sea

Sharif Hazzâ of Mecca, a small man of about fifty years with a dark complexion. His father had been hereditary governor of Mecca, and his older brother had succeeded to the position until Pasha Muhammad Ali of Egypt deposed him.

level, a unique attribute and clear evidence of God's wrath. Scientists of the mid-nineteenth century had judged that the Jordan River had once emptied into the Red Sea, but the volcanic cataclysm that destroyed the five Cities of the Plain—including Sodom and Gomorrah—had closed the opening of the Jordan and created the Dead Sea depression.

Sunday, April 2—In the afternoon, after a religious service that Lynch officiated because the unit had no chaplain,

Lynch attempted to find a solution to the horse problem. He experimented with the single alternative at hand—camels. The obvious solution would be to disassemble the boats into parts, packing each part on a camel. That meant reassembling the boats when they reached the Sea of Galilee, something that could be done . . . but with difficulty. The boats hadn't been disassembled and reassembled, so Lynch didn't know how well that process would work. After all, the reassembled boats might leak.

But then, inspired by a dream the night before (as he wrote later), or maybe relying on knowledge of ancient Middle Eastern army tactics, Lynch hit on the idea of hitching the camels directly to the boat carriages. It sounds obvious enough, but it was an unorthodox idea. Camels were used only as beasts of burden in the contemporary Middle East, never harnessed to pull wagons. The expedition's harnesses, made for horses, were too short, but with modifications, they served the purpose as long as the men kept out of range of the camel's teeth. As they do now, the animals had a nasty tendency to bite anyone who came too close.

Though Lynch didn't know it, Molyneux, in August 1847, transported the dinghy from the HMS *Spartan* cross-country from Acre tied to camels, rather than attempting a cart that restricted him to a smaller boat but allowed him to make better time across the Galilee hills. Molyneux, in contrast to this larger and more elaborate expedition, had only three seamen and Toby, his dragoman and translator. They had no special equipment not already available on the *Spartan* and only letters from the local pasha and assistance from the British vice consul.[81]

At first, the American sailors found that hitching three camels to each carriage, two abreast and one ahead, worked well. Later, they were able to use only two camels per boat, and the men became so familiar with the animals that they decorated their harnesses with ostrich feathers in the way that the Bedouin decorated their horses. Lynch then acquired more camels and horses to carry riders, if not pull a carriage. In all, they headed for the Sea of Galilee with sixteen horses, eleven camels, and a mule.

The camel experiment had educated an eager crowd that gathered to watch. "The successful result taught them something new about the patient and powerful camel, which they thought fit only to plod along with its heavy load upon its back."[82] Indeed, Lynch's use of camels may have been the genesis of an attempt a few years later by the US Army to employ camels in the American West.

After two weeks with the camels, though, Lynch grew disgusted and frustrated. "Of all the burden-bearing beasts, from the Siam elephant to the Himalayan goat, this 'ship of the desert,' as he has been poetically termed,—this clumsy-jointed, splay-footed, wry-neck, vicious camel, with his look of injured innocence, and harsh, complaining voice, is incomparably the most disagreeable."[83] No doubt the camels weren't terribly fond of him either.

The American sailors, in a caravan with the two metal boats mounted on carriages and a few Arabs including a dragoman and Mustafa, the cook, turned their backs on the bay at Acre and headed east, moving at the slow rhythm set by the swaying, disagreeable camels. Following what might be better described as a camel track or horse trail than a proper road, they left the coastal plain and headed into the sparsely settled low hills and valleys.

Soon they would reach the Galilee mountains, a rugged barrier between the sea on the west, and the Jordan Rift

The expedition caravan, using camels to pull the boats, leaves Acre and sets out across the desert plain for the Sea of Galilee.

Valley, a fault line bordered on the west by high plateaus. Through the Jordan Rift Valley, often called the Ghor, flowed the Jordan River, which would lead them through lands of unknown and perhaps hostile Bedouin tribes, followed by the desolation of the Dead Sea. Their circuitous route would take them to Jerusalem, fulfilling a dream of a lifetime for Lynch and the sailors. Much was uncertain, but in Galilee, its hills tinted purple and gray at sunset, all knew that adventure lay ahead.

But first, because the caravan would pass nearby, Lynch was invited to visit Sheikh 'Akil in his mountain fortress. Lynch intended to invite the sheikh and his men along on their Dead Sea quest. Better to have the powerful Bedouin chieftain as an ally than as an adversary, considering the untold challenges that lay ahead in the wilds of Palestine.

IV

Cross-country with Bedouin

Even before the expedition left the beach at Acre, the officers began taking longitude and latitude measurements for the maps that the expedition would produce of Palestine, the Jordan River, and the Dead Sea. There wasn't a lack of maps of Palestine at the time. Blank spaces still existed on maps of other parts of the world, such as the Amazon, but not on those of this region. Indeed, that was the problem.

The many maps made by the Christian West, going back thousands of years, depicted the biblical Palestine—or rather what people imagined the biblical Palestine was like. Even when a map claimed to show modern Palestine, much of it derived from lore and the stories of travelers. The only previous systematic latitude and longitude measurements were those that the French army surveyors made during

Napoleon's campaign in 1799 and the ones that British military engineers prepared in 1841. In both cases, the measurements were fragmentary—which unfortunately didn't stop cartographers from using them, combined with hearsay, to create maps that proved less than helpful.

Lynch and his officers used their new French sextants to measure latitude, their north-south position, determined by the height of the North Star or the angle of the noon sun above the horizon. Longitude—the east-west coordinate—they also measured. Until the eighteenth century, longitude had been impossible to ascertain accurately. Scientists struggled for hundreds of years to find a way to compute it, for without knowing a ship's longitude, captains, thinking they were miles from shore, often ran their ships onto reefs, accidentally sinking them. Some tried comparing the relative position of Mars and the moon; others looked to the phases of Jupiter's moons. The invention of the chronometer, an extremely accurate timepiece, finally solved the problem so that local position could be compared with a reference meridian.

Lynch planned to fix latitude and longitude calculations at least once per day while traveling, and several times more when camped. Otherwise, the lieutenants, experienced draftsmen, filled in the contours of their maps by recording their observations of the terrain.

Tuesday, April 4—The caravan, with boats mounted on carriages pulled by camels, American sailors on horseback, and a few Arabs, including the cook, made for the coastal plain and the low mountains ahead. Caravan routes ran north and south along the coastline, connecting Beirut and points north and west with Egypt, but roads that ran east and west in ancient times had disappeared by the mid-nineteenth century. The tracks that the American expedition followed were used by men on horseback and by loaded camels, not wheels, so the carriages bearing the boats slowed progress to a crawl over rocks and ruts.

While the expedition caravan inched cross-country toward the Jordan, Lieutenant Lynch, at Sheikh 'Akil's invitation, rode ahead to visit him in his mountain fortress, 'Ibillin, on the route across Galilee.[84] Knowing little about 'Akil apart from their brief meetings—his colorful garb, curved sword, status as a sheikh—Lynch was apprehensive. But the sheikh captivated Lynch, who intuitively sensed his leadership skills. He accepted the invitation, even if it put his life in danger, because he wanted to prevail upon the sheikh to accompany the expedition and didn't want to make a show of distrust. As a precaution, he left a letter for Lt. John Dale, his second in command, telling him, "If I should not return, push on, without delay, to the Jordan and the Dead Sea and accomplish the objects of the expedition."[85]

On his sure-footed horse, Lynch followed one of 'Akil's tribesman as he veered off the level plain, taking a shortcut, and headed up a steep, rough, winding track. As they reached the hills, the landscape displayed an impressive wealth of plants and flowers, both beautiful and fragrant—"The white and crimson aster, the pale asphodel, the scarlet anemone, the blue and purple convolvulus, the cyclamen, and others resembling the eglantine rose."[86] Finally they reached 'Ibillin, a village perched on the highest peak in sight, giving it a magnificent vantage point. 'Akil's fortress sat in a well defensible location, protected by a ravine that made it look, to Lynch's eyes, like an inaccessible lion's hold.

Unfortunately, the natural beauty of the setting contrasted sharply with the poverty and filth of the village itself. One-story stone houses built without mortar had mud roofs. The residents cooked their bread in small, dome-roofed outdoor ovens also made of baked earth. The fragrant smell of the bread mixed with the putrid odor of burning dried camel excrement that the inhabitants used for fuel.

After dismounting, Lynch waited in an open courtyard until one of the Bedouin led him into a large, mud-floored room with stained rafters. Smoke rose from a pile of smoldering embers in the center of the room, darkening the ceiling. No chimney vented the smoke. The usual coffee pot—small and dirty, made of brass—simmered in the embers. 'Akil sat at the far end of the room, surrounded by some of his followers who, like their sheikh, were armed to the teeth with curved swords, all very much in evidence. Sharif Hazzâ was also present, though Lynch hadn't expected to see him again so soon.

Everyone sat in awkward silence. Lynch didn't speak Arabic, nor did any of the Bedouin know English. Lynch had come alone, so there was no translator. Everywhere Lynch looked, eyes held to him. When he turned his attention from one place to another, their eyes followed his movement. Customarily, the host would break the silence by offering his guest coffee and a pipe. Even though Lynch wouldn't have understood the words, he had been in Palestine long enough to be able to read symbolic gestures of hospitality—or the lack of them. Ominously, the friendship offering didn't come. No coffee, no pipe. The sharif, whom Lynch thought friendly, didn't break the silence either. Instead, he

seemed lost in thought, staring at the lit coal powering his water pipe.

Lynch motioned, acknowledging 'Akil's presence, to which the sheikh responded with a corresponding gesture—but without warmth. Still no offer of coffee and pipe. 'Akil's followers exchanged glances and a few brief words that Lynch recognized, mostly *lah,* the Arabic word for *no.* Was the visit a trap? Lynch began to worry for his safety. Then the group started an animated discussion. Occasionally one of the speakers looked toward him uneasily as if wondering why he had earned such a cool reception. Lynch began to speculate that the Bedouin were planning to rob him. They might suspect correctly that he carried a large sum of money to finance the expedition.

Growing impatient, Lynch pulled out his pocket watch to see the time. Instantly, the conversation paused, and the sheikh asked to see the instrument. The Bedouin crowded around, as Lynch described, "like so many wild Indians for the first time beholding a mirror"—the first of many times that he compared the Bedouin to Native Americans.[87] Relishing the moment, Lynch slowly exhibited the watch's features, which included a winding key. When the group grew bored, he drew his officer's sword and displayed the peculiar handle with the built-in rifle barrels. About the time the group tired of all of Lynch's possessions, he heard the sounds of the expedition's caravan approaching.

Relieved, Lynch sprang to his feet, shouting, *"Djemmell!"* —camel.[88]

Voices from the caravan echoed, "Djemmell! Djemmell!" and the Bedouin's attitude shifted as they saw the arrival of the American sailors and the boats pulled by camels. Lynch felt instantly safe, knowing that the carbines of his troop, along with the blunderbuss, would outgun any weapons the Bedouin might have. 'Akil drew Lynch aside and, through the translator who arrived with the caravan, privately offered an excuse for the cool reception: An emissary of Sa'id Bey was present, and 'Akil hadn't wanted to disclose his plans to join the expedition in front of him. Lynch didn't know whether to believe the excuse. If the caravan hadn't arrived when it did, what might have happened? Would he have been robbed? Held prisoner? Would he be dead?

Ancestors of the Bedouin tribes had migrated from the Arabian Peninsula between the fourteenth and eighteenth centuries. Their lives changed little until the second quarter of the twentieth century, and, as Lynch correctly portrayed them, the Bedouin lived largely outside the Ottomans' ability to govern or control. Bedouin society functioned through a code of honor that demanded loyalty first to the clan and then to the tribe. The hospitality of the Bedouin was legendary; their code dictated that no traveler went away hungry or thirsty. But the tribe also used penalties of exile or blood money, as well as all-out vengeance, to maintain their social order.

It was indeed curious that 'Akil didn't serve Lynch refreshment, even if an emissary of Sa'id Bey was watching. Lynch speculated later that if robbery were intended, he had arrived before the plans were complete. Or perhaps the arrival of the sharif disrupted their plans since the tribesmen might not have been certain of the older gentleman's reaction. In any case, once 'Akil and the sharif told Lynch they would join the expedition, and once they offered coffee and a water pipe, according to custom, the agreement was inviolate. 'Akil and his Bedouin followers would neither rob nor harm Lynch or his men.

Lynch rejoined the expedition's caravan, leaving the Bedouin to follow once they had organized their outerwear and weapons for the desert, including long, flowing *abas* (cloaks) and yellow keffiyehs, the woven-check cotton scarves held to the head with dyed-black cords of camel's hair. Looking the part of wild and savage warriors, each carried a spear eighteen feet long, frequently decorated with ostrich feathers.

The caravan headed due east to east-southeast, then turned gradually to the south into the Wadi en Nafakh (Blowing Valley) where they halted—though it was barely three o'clock in the afternoon. Water regulates life in the desert, not time, so they stopped for the night near a well, rather than venturing farther toward an area of rough and arid terrain that would prove a challenge for transporting the boats. As both groups set up camp, one of the Bedouin brought in a sheep to butcher for dinner and share between the men. Lynch accepted the fresh meat gratefully, not querying whence it came. The Bedouin would make fine guides and traveling companions, he decided, and he rejoiced at securing their services.

Lynch arranged the camp to be easily defended. The tents and the carriages holding the boats formed a sort of breastwork, not unlike the way frontiersmen in the American West circled their wagons to protect against Native attacks. Behind the boats and the tents, the Americans arranged their camels and horses. The American flag was flying, and, just beyond, an officer and two sailors with carbines guarded the camp, the loaded blunderbuss on a stand between them. Farther away, the Bedouin had pitched a blue tent, their lances, tufted with ostrich feathers, stuck into the ground before it.

The Bedouin horses, much superior beasts to the Americans', stood tethered nearby. The old sharif had a splendid gray mare, while the sheikh and most of his followers rode beautiful bay mares. Also among them were two jet-black Nubians. One of the Bedouin horsemen, with flowing robes and long lance, was posted as a lookout about half a mile from the camp. Lynch watched with appreciation as the man's silhouette stood against the sky.

Wednesday, April 5—As they rode along the plain, the Bedouin entertained the Americans by demonstrating their magnificent horsemanship. They plunged about, twirling their long spears, suddenly charging upon and then barely avoiding each other. It might have been a game played back home, except that, instead of the familiar short and blunted spear of a game, the Bedouin played with long, sharp-pointed weapons of war.

Later in the day, the caravan reached a region of broken and rocky ground, little more than a mule track. Wheeled carriages clearly had never before traversed it. Now Lynch understood why the French, in their 1799 invasion, had not tried to wheel their guns and gun-carriages across the terrain. They had taken them apart and transported them on the backs of camels over the rugged rock ridges and only mounted them again when they reached the level plain.

That evening, the Americans visited the Bedouin in their nearby tent to feast on another sheep. Lynch wrote patronizingly of the encounter: "What a patriarchal scene! Seated upon their mats and cushions within, we looked out upon

the fire, around which were gathered groups of this wild people, who continually reminded us of our Indians." He described their evening meal, probably *mansuf*, the traditional Bedouin dish: "A whole sheep, entombed in rice, which they pitched into without knives or forks, in the most amusing manner." Meanwhile, a minstrel "twanged away upon his instrument" and chanted Arabic poetry that, of course, the Americans didn't understand.[89] Both groups ended the evening by agreeing that they would reach the Sea of Galilee the next day—*Inshallah!* If God wills it.

Some Native American tribes did possess similarities to the Bedouin: They lived nomadic lives beyond the control of the established government. Courageous warriors and magnificent horsemen, they won grudging respect as fighters from encroaching Europeans, who considered them inferior. While Lynch's expedition mingled with Bedouin, and he compared them to Native Americans, the Indian Wars continued unabated in the United States, Manifest Destiny providing a convenient excuse, if not an imperative, to crowd out or remove natives from desirable land.

The next day dawned clear in Palestine, the sun rising cloudlessly over the eastern hills as Lynch called all hands, breakfasted, and struck the tents. To the boat carriages the sailors hitched the camels. The expedition headed east, downhill, then up and down over the undulations of the rolling plain and hills. They hadn't seen a tree for days, but the valley was fertile, carpeted with growing grain and patches of flowers. The scarlet anemone and the blue convolvulus, combined with the green fields, made a mosaic of the landscape, studded with thorns. Peasants in ragged clothing worked the fields, though no houses came into view. The caravan did pass straggling groups of Bedouin, also on the road, who saluted the group in a friendly fashion.

Here, and several more times in Lynch's narrative about the expedition, he remarked upon the untapped potential of the region for agriculture. The prospect of cotton particularly interested him as a southerner. He even imagined a thriving cotton culture supported by freed slaves transported from the United States, an idea that he believed could provide a solution to America's worsening slavery problem.[90] As he proceeded through Palestine, over and over he noted fertile fields cultivated minimally or not at all. His idea of freed slaves in Palestine never happened, but the Civil War inadvertently did prove a boon to Palestinian agriculture, with grain and cotton exported in greatly increased amounts through the war years.

In the mid-afternoon they passed a crater-like series of slopes and then caught a glimpse of the Sea of Galilee in the far distance. They continued along the northern ridge of the valley and in half an hour crossed the road between Jerusalem and Damascus where they found a group of Christian pilgrims resting around a fountain and drinking from it. The group's horses, heads drooping, waited their turn for a chance to drink. Lynch and his men didn't stop to talk but continued at a slow pace, burdened as they were by the metal boats. Another small party passed the Americans, including a young Syrian girl. Lynch remarked that she was the only pretty female they had seen in Palestine so far, noting her smooth, bronze-tinted skin and pleasing features.

But having seen a glimpse of the sea, he surrendered to impatience, riding ahead for another viewing. The body of water, more accurately a lake than a sea, shimmered like a mirror, nestled in the rounded and green but treeless hills around it. "How dear to the Christian are the memories of that lake! Blessed beyond the nature of its element, it has borne the Son of God upon its surface. Its cliffs first echoed the glad tidings of salvation, and from its villages the first of the apostles were gathered to the ministry."[91]

Then he realized that he was standing close to the Mount of Beatitudes, the hill overlooking the Sea of Galilee where Jesus preached the Sermon on the Mount. Woe was the man, Lynch believed, who questioned the locations of blessed events such as the Mount of Beatitudes and failed to feel reverence for hallowed ground. "Away with such hard-hearted skepticism," he proclaimed. What does it matter "whether in this field or an adjoining one—on this mount, or another more or less contiguous to it, the Savior exhorted, blessed, or fed his followers?"[92] It was better to draw inspiration and awe from the whole of the experience rather than waste the trip in geographical skepticism.

Many Americans might have fantasized about the Holy Land before they arrived, but it was a real, touchable place.[93] For Lynch, Palestine was so much more than a neglected backwater of the Ottoman Empire, so much more than the Roman or Byzantine ruins scattered everywhere around. The meaning and power invested in the place, though, didn't exist in current reality, but only in the imagined connections of places with incidents from its biblical past.

As Lynch descended the steep hill toward the lake, he returned to practicalities. He asked himself: "How in the world are the boats ever to be got down this rocky and precipitous path, when we are compelled to alight and lead our horses?"[94] From Acre they dragged the boats up and down valleys and ridges, but from where he was standing, down to the sea was a steep, almost sheer descent. Once they dealt with this slope, though it might be a desperate effort, they would be able to launch their boats, and the Americans could return as sailors to their natural element—water.

He and some of the sailors temporarily left the boats beside a fountain before they traversed the steep descent and continued into the town of Tiberias on the Sea of Galilee. Heavily damaged by an earthquake in 1837, ruins of what once had been stately structures ringed the shore, and the city wall had collapsed. Little progress had been made in rebuilding, though Jews from America and Europe had begun sending donations to aid the rebuilding effort. During the 1840s, a temporary loosening of Ottoman restrictions allowed some Jews from around the world to immigrate to Palestine. Some came to help rebuild Tiberias, though the immigration movement wouldn't acquire the Zionist name and identity until later in the century. Despite its damaged condition, Tiberias still commanded particular reverence for the Jews because they believed that Jacob had resided there and hoped that the messiah would rise from the shores of the lake.

Lynch brought letters of introduction to the chief rabbi, who came to greet them. The rabbi escorted them through twisted, damaged streets to the home of Heim Wiseman, who ran it as a rooming house at the suggestion of an earlier traveler, Prince Puckler-Muskau from Silesia, who had employed Wiseman as a guide.[95] Wiseman showed Lynch a register with a message written in English, Italian, and very bad Spanish that asked visitors, when they were ready to depart, to leave whatever money they thought appropriate to pay for their accommodations in his house-hotel. This clear expression of hospitality and graciousness impressed

The American expedition visited Tiberias, the ancient city on the Sea of Galilee that had suffered severe damage in an 1837 earthquake.

Lynch. How much better was that arrangement than the abhorrent haggling over price.

The sharif and sheikh surprised Lynch when they appeared at Wiseman's. Lynch concluded that only their kind feelings toward the Americans had induced them to enter the home of a Jew. The group, with the two Muslim leaders, received three other rabbis who came to call, but Sharif Hazzâ and Sheikh 'Akil treated the rabbis with respect. When Muslim visitors joined the group, the sharif and the sheikh greeted them with an embrace. The visitors included the governor of the town, a relative of 'Akil's, with whom the sharif and sheikh soon left to lodge.

The next day, accompanied by Wiseman, who showed him the way to the governor's residence, Lynch returned the governor's visit. Upon arrival, Wiseman sat down on the floor while the others rested on the divan. After a servant served sherbet to the Muslims and to Lynch, he offered a glass to Wiseman, who refused, as it was the eve of the Feast of the Azymes, the celebration of the Jews' release from Egyptian bondage, a strict fast day for him. The servant exclaimed at the refusal, and the governor abruptly told Wiseman to drink it. "The poor Jew, agitated and trembling, carried it to his lips," said Lynch, "where he held it for a moment, when, perceiving the attention of the governor to be diverted, he put down the untasted goblet."[96]

After meeting with the governor, Wiseman, ever courteous to the Americans, led Lynch to a chapel dedicated to St. Peter, said to be built on the spot where Jesus performed a miracle, causing Lynch to muse over the strangeness that a Jew should point out a holy place of a religion he denied. When they returned to Wiseman's house, Lynch noticed with some amusement that the sailors were enjoying the temporary novelty of having a roof over their heads. The Americans relished the delicious fish from the lake for supper, while locals gathered around to watch and laugh at the Americans' peculiar manner of eating with metal utensils—a reversal of the Americans' reaction at seeing the Bedouin eat with their fingers. Tired but gratified, the Americans lay down to sleep—but discovered that fleas were sharing their beds with them.

Saturday, April 8, rose to a beautiful, calm morning, a good day to launch the boats that the expedition had towed twenty-five miles in five days. But first, Lynch had to enlist the whole party, Americans and Bedouin, to bring the boats down the side of the mountain from where they had left them beside the fountain. The group occasionally had to resort to ropes to lower the boats over a precipice. As they slowly progressed, Lynch pondered that, if the ropes broke, "like the herd of swine in the Bible, they would rush precipitately into the sea."[97] The ropes didn't break, however, and at length he proudly noted that the boats were "carried beyond the walls uninjured and, amid a crowd of spectators, launched upon the blue waters of the Sea of Galilee."[98]

Interestingly, an anonymous sailor's narrative published about the expedition says that the boats arrived damaged, requiring the use of American hammers that echoed over the lake.[99] Perhaps Lynch wanted to recall nothing but perfection for such an auspicious moment when American boats launched on that consecrated body of water. Lynch believed that no vessel of any size had sailed on the sea since the time of Josephus and the Romans, and, so far as he could ascertain, only one frail wooden rowboat then plied the lake.

Lynch purchased the boat to use for transporting the expedition's tents and other gear and christened it with the grandiose name *Uncle Sam.* He didn't want to take time to explore the lake then, as it would delay their arrival at the Dead Sea, so he arranged for another wooden boat to be built. Thus, the sailors would be able to explore the lake on their return trip from Jerusalem to Beirut after they explored the Dead Sea.

As the boats slid onto the lake, the Bedouin sang, clapping their hands, and the locals cried for baksheesh, the often-repeated request for money that all foreigners faced in the Middle East. The dignified Americans neither shouted nor cheered, however, for in the context of the blessed Sea of Galilee, cheering from Christian lips would sound like profanity. Just looking at the lake, wrote Lynch, "soothed for a time all worldly care." The two *Fannies* floated buoyantly, flying the Stars and Stripes, which the Americans thought the "the noblest flag of freedom now waving in the world."[100]

All rested at peace a short time before starting the next chapter of their journey—rest they would need, for the arduous weeks ahead contained both a religious quest and a physical mission.

V

Down the Jordan

In 1805, Ulrich Seetzen, an Arabic-speaking German physician, covered himself in his old *kombaz* or dressing gown and added a ragged blue shift. He wrapped his head with shreds of old cloth, slipped his feet into worn slippers, and threw a tattered aba over his shoulders. Claiming a branch of a tree as a walking stick, he set off from Tiberias into the cold and rain. Thus garbed, without guide or provisions, he became the first European to rediscover the remnants of Greco-Roman civilization in Palestine—the wealthy Decapolis cities that no westerner had seen since ancient times. By donning the dress of a common beggar, he hoped to avoid the attention of marauding Bedouin and overzealous Ottoman officials. The slippers pinched his feet, though, so after a few miles he decided to leave them beside the road, walking in the mud barefoot.

Seetzen had already tried exploring in his usual European dress, first on horseback with guides and bearing a firman from the pasha of Damascus. In less than a week, though, Turkish horsemen took him prisoner, and a local army officer held him on suspicion of possessing forged papers. After his release, he escaped a Bedouin attack only because of his guide's quick thinking. A month later, Seetzen tried again, this time disguised as an undistinguished Bedouin sheikh on a mule, with muleteers and a Greek Orthodox guide known to have connections with the Aneze, a confederation of Bedouin tribes.

With these companions, he traveled south and watched hunters flush out wild boar by setting fire to the rushes of the Huleh marshes. Eventually, though, the disguise failed as guides deserted him and others robbed him. Yet he managed to discover the ruins of Caesarea Philippi and one of the sources of the Jordan River. But by the time he reached Tiberias on foot, he was grateful to be alive. The only way to survive, he decided—as seasoned travelers will tell you— was to travel with nothing worth stealing.

The lost Decapolis cities, the ten legendary trade metropolises of the Greco-Roman world, had formed a line along the flourishing trade route between Damascus, in the north, and the lost city of Philadelphia, to the south, somewhere in the hills east of the Dead Sea. Did they still exist, even in remnants, their fertile fields still tilled? Or had they disappeared into the desert, swallowed by sand and time? No westerner knew for sure until Seetzen searched for them that winter.

During his wanderings, he shared meals of gruel made of wheat, rice, and wild herbs with villagers and slept in caves with peasants' goats. While with Bedouin, he pretended to be Muslim; when with Greek Orthodox peasants, he claimed to be of their faith. In his beggar guise, Seetzen circled the Dead Sea, which no other foreigner would try for many years. In his travels, he rediscovered three Decapolis cities for the West: Gadara, overlooking the Sea of Galilee; Gerasa (Jerash) with its Corinthian columns, temples, and Roman theater; and Philadelphia, now Amman, the capital city of Jordan.

Seetzen was also the first European to travel with Bible in hand—not for divine inspiration but to extract descriptions of the landscape. He used these descriptions, combined with Arab place names and his own intuition, to deduce locations mentioned in the Old Testament.[101]

Jean-Louis Burckhardt, a proud Swiss exile, studied Arabic and Oriental culture in Leipzig and Heidelberg before moving to England and falling in with Sir Joseph Banks and other explorers. Like Seetzen, Burckhardt began his 1809 Middle Eastern travels on horseback, using the region as a training ground for explorations in Africa, though both died before embarking on their planned explorations there. Also like Seetzen, he avoided the major trade and pilgrimage routes, instead riding from village to village, observing and asking questions of the peasants when he could avoid raising suspicion.

In 1812, on a trip from Damascus to search for the lost city of Petra in the desert wilderness near the Dead Sea, Burckhardt wanted to retrace Seetzen's route down the east side of the Jordan. His guides, though, took flight at

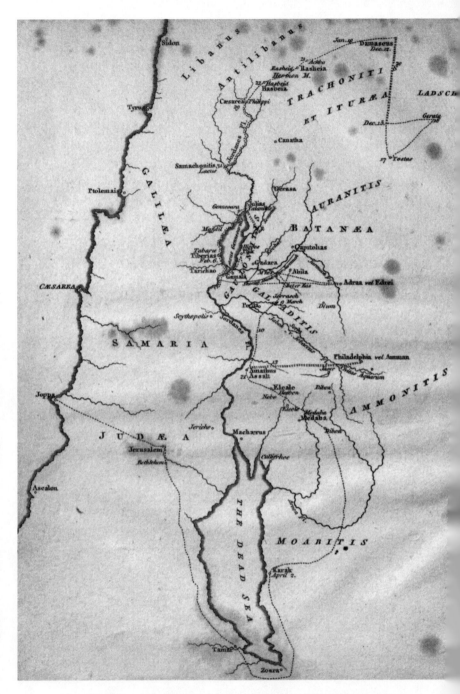

Map of Palestine, based on Ulrich Seetzen's travels in 1808–09 that included
walking around the Dead Sea. *Courtesy of HathiTrust.*

the sight of a fresh horse's footprint—such was the state of unrest in the countryside. Hearing that the sheikh of Kerak and his entourage were heading south on the east side of the river, he hastened to join the retinue for protection. The cunning sheikh, however, tricked Burckhardt out of his expensive Damascus saddle. Burckhardt then sold his horse for some corn and four goats that he used to pay a peasant family to take him through the desert. When the family spied marauding Bedouin, though, they canceled the arrangement. Only when another sheikh intervened was he able to get his goats back.

No guides were willing to take him to Petra because they thought foreigners wanted the treasure rumored to be buried in the ruins. Burckhardt tricked one devout Muslim into taking him by telling the man that he wanted to sacrifice a goat at the tomb of Aaron, the brother of Moses, knowing that the guide would revere such a task. Burckhardt knew the legend that Aaron's tomb overlooked the Wadi Musa, where Petra was rumored to be. The guide reluctantly agreed and led him on the only route to the tomb, which took them through the narrow, curving valley that wound past magnificent tombs carved into the rock face.

When Burckhardt stopped to marvel at the beauty of the red rock city, the guide grew suspicious. "I see now clearly that you are an infidel, who has some particular business amongst the ruins of the city of your forefathers, but depend upon it, we shall not suffer you to take out one para [smallest coin] of the treasures hidden there, for they are in our territory, and belong to us."[102] Burckhardt denied the accusation, but, fearing the guide would rob and abandon him in the desert, he didn't linger among the ruins as he wanted. Instead, he hastened with the man to Aaron's tomb and choked down the unwanted, hastily cooked meat of a sacrificed goat.

After several instances of being robbed and tricked by guides, sheikhs, and Bedouin tribes, Burckhardt came to agree with Seetzen about the advisability of disguise as a beggar:

> *Travels in these countries, if extended beyond the great caravan routes, admit only two modes to ensure the traveler's safety. He must either travel with a Pasha's retinue to ensure his safety . . . or else he must throw himself, as an object of compassion, upon the mercy and good-natured disposition of the natives. Any half measures cannot fail to expose him to embarrassment and danger.*[103]

Despite the adventures of Seetzen, Burckhardt, and a handful of other European explorers, the interior of Palestine, except for Nazareth, Jerusalem, and Bethlehem, still represented, in 1848, *terra incognita* for westerners. Even among holy cities, Greek Orthodox, Armenian, and other Eastern Christians outnumbered Catholic and Protestant pilgrims from the West.

It had been a commonplace belief for centuries that Palestine—once mighty, now fallen; once glorious, now obscure—had descended into its ruined state as punishment for deicide, the killing of Jesus. Those few Western Christians who ventured to the Holy Land found nothing to compare to the Parthenon or the Pyramids, and the bazaars couldn't compete with those of Damascus or Alexandria. Moreover, the real Holy Land couldn't even compete with itself as depicted in the glorious images painted by European masters.

True, Napoleon's invasion in 1799 had reawakened the West to Palestine's existence, and the continued Napoleonic Wars in Europe caused wealthy travelers to look farther east than to Italy for their destinations. But knowledge, in the form of observed reality, had yet to displace myth and legend so far as the Jordan River and the Ghor were concerned.

Lynch may have read excerpts of Seetzen's work, though the journals and letters of the latter didn't appear in their entirety until the 1850s. Lynch would have read Burckhardt's *Travels in Syria and the Holy Land* with interest. Lynch may even have taken particular note of what the editor—not Burckhardt, who was dead by then—said in the book's introduction. The extended length of the Jordan River Valley—the Ghor—indicates that the "Jordan once discharged itself into the Red Sea, and confirm[s] the truth of that great volcanic convulsion, described in the nineteenth chapter of Genesis, which interrupted the course of the river." The cataclysmic event converted the lake into the Dead Sea and "the fertile plain occupied by the cities of Adma, Zeboin, Sodom, and Gomorrah . . . into a sandy desert."[104] This editorial statement was the stuff of religion not observation. However, it was exactly what Lynch hoped to prove by his journey down the Jordan.

In a way Lynch did take Burckhardt's rather colorful advice—to wear a disguise while exploring Palestine. Certainly, in the guise of American navy uniforms, Lynch and his men were neither beggars sleeping with farmers' goats nor a pasha's retinue with its hand-knotted Turkish rugs, gilt cups, and perfumed bathing water. But their appearance certainly bewildered with its unfamiliarity. Moreover, the ostentation of their blunderbuss and pistol-enhanced swords and knives, as well as their choice of traveling companions—sharif and sheikh—intimidated as much as would any pasha's retinue. Whether it would deter the Bedouin who attacked Molyneux and others, though, they had yet to determine.

Alexander Kinglake, author of the popular 1844 travel narrative *Eothen: Traces of Travel Brought Home from the East*, wrote that on the bank of the Jordan, "you are upon the very frontier of all accustomed respectabilities. There, on the other side of the river . . . reigns the people that will be like to put you to death, for *not* being a vagrant, for *not* being a robber, for *not* being armed and houseless."[105] Weary of polite European society, Kinglake relished the romantic notion of travel in dangerous regions. Lynch's men also no doubt welcomed the hazards they wanted courageously to overcome.

But the reality of the river that lay ahead was unknown to them, for there were no accurate maps or verified verbal accounts of its progress. Kinglake wrote that the "course of the Jordan is from the north to the south, and in that direction, with very little of devious winding, it carries the shining waters of Galilee straight down to the solitudes of the Dead Sea."[106] Leading scientific authorities in Britain, such as the president of the Royal Geographical Society of London, William Hamilton, hypothesized that the Jordan River fell nearly one thousand feet between the Sea of Galilee and the Dead Sea. In his president's address in 1843, Hamilton asserted, "There still remains to be executed in this part of the globe a very important and interesting operation, to account for the very great discrepancy."[107]

Puzzled at the prospect of the river's drop in altitude, Edward Robinson compared the fall of the Jordan to that of the Elbe, Danube, and Rhine. If the river were as straight as Kinglake claimed, anyone trying to navigate it would have serious problems. Robinson calculated that, unless the Jordan meandered a great deal more than travelers reported or unless it had extensive rapids, three or more sets of Niagara-like falls could lay hidden in the Palestinian wilderness—and the current still ran as fast as the swiftest portion of the Rhine.[108]

Yet neither Costigan nor Molyneux, who Lynch knew had descended the Jordan, had mentioned tourist-worthy waterfalls. How the river absorbed that thousand-foot fall in altitude remained a mystery solvable only one way—by exiting the Sea of Galilee and seeing what happened next.

~

Monday, April 10—The lake narrowed as the boats approached its southern end. To the southwest they spied the ruins of Taricheae or Al Majdal, thought to be the biblical town of Magdala, birthplace of Mary Magdalene. To the east, a green plain sloped down to the lake, which curved to the west at that point into a ravine, or wadi as the Arabs called them, about three-quarters of a mile wide.

About mid-afternoon, the boats approached a dense thicket, the shade from which almost hid where the Sea of Galilee diverged into the Jordan River. Indeed, when Molyneux passed that way in his dinghy the previous year, Toby, his dragoman, had to run along the bank to point the way to the lake outlet, which looked like another place where the lakeshore curved into a small inlet. The water flowed so slowly that Molyneux couldn't differentiate it from ripples of wind on the lake. The water that flowed some thirty feet wide from the lake into the wadi was clear as crystal, not muddy with sediment, as it had been when it entered the north end of the lake.[109]

As the American sailors crossed the imaginary line between the Sea of Galilee and the Jordan River, they felt the same sense of reverent but intense excitement as when they had launched the boats. "Before us was the stream which, God willing, would lead us to our wondrous destination— the Dead Sea."[110]

The boats of the American expedition floated and paddled down the Jordan River, which flows through the Jordan Rift Valley, also called the Ghor.

The Jordan Rift Valley, through which the river flowed, sometimes to the western side and sometimes to the eastern side of a narrow plain, forms a deep crevasse called the Ghor. Robinson thought that the Jordan once may have overflowed its banks yearly, like the Nile, flooding this plain, but he could find no evidence to prove it. Beyond the narrow plain, the sides of the valley rose like rough walls. Barren mountains then skirted the valley, stretching away in the distance, their southern extremities half hidden or lost in a faint purple haze that partially obscured their extent.

Lynch and his sailors, accompanied by their Arab allies, headed downriver through one of the world's most distinctive ecosystems toward the lowest point on Earth. With awnings spread and colors flying, Lynch led the way in the *Fanny Mason*. Midshipman Aulick followed in the *Fanny Skinner*. *Uncle Sam*, repaired only that morning to a barely seaworthy state and sailed by Arab boatmen, brought up the rear. Soon the lake slipped from sight. "I assigned to myself, in the *Fanny Mason*," Lynch wrote, "the course, rapidity, color, and depth of the river and its tributaries,—the nature of its banks, and of the country through which it flowed,—the vegetable productions, and the birds and animals we might see, with a journal of events."[111]

To Aulick, who had charge of the *Fanny Skinner*, he assigned the topographical sketching of the river and its shores. Only the deadline of reaching the Dead Sea before the worst of the summer heat bore down upon them prevented them from using more precise fixed-station mapping technology.

Using those instruments, they would have had to stop at every turn of the river. A man in the lead boat would stand on shore and hold a rod marked with a sighting point. Someone in the following boat would beach that boat and set up the Troughton spirit level on a tripod to measure the horizontal and vertical angle of the change in the river's path from that spot to the lead boat's sighting point. This more careful surveying method would have slowed the expedition's progress to a glacial pace, so they made do instead with Aulick's estimates of the river's path, as confirmed by Lieutenant Dale's topographical sketches from shore.

Now that they were fully on the river, some seventy-five feet wide, one of the sailors cast the log over the side and allowed the line attached to it to play out over his fingers. The line had knots every forty-seven feet and three inches. Another sailor held a thirty-second sandglass, and when the time had passed they could tell the speed of the water by how many knots had played out. The current was flowing at two knots (two nautical miles per hour), or approximately 2.3 land miles per hour.

Due to the river's curves, they lost sight of the lake within five minutes of leaving it. The rounded riverbanks rose thirty feet from the valley floor, much more inviting than the craggy mountains in the distance. Though without trees or bushes, the riverbanks were covered with a verdant mix of grass and flowers, which Lynch identified as "scarlet anemone, the yellow marigold, and occasionally a water-lily, and here and there a straggling asphodel."[112]

One sailor pointed westward where they caught a glimpse of the shore party, some thirty strong: "Eleven camels stalked solemnly ahead, followed by the wild Bedouin on their blooded animals, with their abas flying in the wind, and their long gun-barrels glittering in the sun; and Lieutenant Dale and his officers in the Frank costume brought up the rear."[113] Lieutenant Dale commanded the shore party, which included Sheikh 'Akil and ten of his tribesmen, all heavily armed. 'Akil retained his curved sword and wore a green aba, red hat and boots, and flowing white trousers. Only Sharif Hazzâ rode unarmed due to his "priestly character."

With them came Emir Nasser 'Arar el Ghuzzhawy, sheikh of the El Ghuzzarlyeh tribe, who heard of the expedition and the eminence of the Americans' Arab friends. Offering his services, el Ghuzzhawy and his companions, in their flowing robes, some dark, some white or red, escorted the expedition through their tribal lands. Impressed with the emir's power, Lynch praised the size and fertility of his territory, comparing it to "some of the petty kingdoms of Europe." He later described el Ghuzzhawy, whom he somewhat unkindly nicknamed the "ogre prince," as

> *considerably taller and stouter than the generality of the race; his complexion was of the tint of burnt umber, his eye black, lascivious, and glistening like that of a snake; he wore a tangled black beard, and, with his fang-like teeth, smiled. . . . His costume was in no manner distinguished from that of his numerous attendants, unless in its superlative uncleanliness.*[114]

Lynch detailed Lieutenant Dale to "make topographical sketches of the country as he proceeded, and such other notes as circumstances would permit."[115] Dr. Anderson was directed to make geological observations and to collect mineral specimens. Lynch asked Mr. Bedlow to record any incidents that occurred to the land party and the nature of the countryside they traveled and his son, Francis, to collect plants and flowers.

According to Lynch's instructions, the shore party was "to keep as near to the river as the nature of the country would permit, and should they hear two guns fired in quick succession, to leave the camel-drivers to take care of themselves, and hasten with all speed to our assistance. I felt sure that Mr. Dale would not fail me, and in that respect my mind was at ease."[116] Mounted Bedouin scouts fanned out in three directions ahead of the shore party, but, even so, what paths they could find often lay five hundred feet or more from the valley floor.

The Arab leaders—Sheikh 'Akil, Sharif Hazzâ, and Emir el Ghuzzhawy—all agreed that the well-armed shore caravan would not be in any danger. An attack upon the boats while they were entangled in rocks or rapids and out of sight of the shore party posed the only real fear. In that case, rifle shots were the only means of communication.

The boats passed a low island, ninety yards long and tufted with shrubbery on the left, then another marshy one on the right. Lynch estimated the depth of the clear water at ten feet. To the north, the snow on Mount Hermon glittered. The current flowed slowly but moved along, so the sailors, instead of rowing, used the oars to direct the boats toward the deep channel of the river. Even still, their passage frightened into flight waterfowl in the reeds on the sides of the river and on the marshy island.

Then a shot broke the tranquility of the slow-moving river. This was the agreed-upon signal for danger, though the cause for the shot was not yet clear. Had the shore party been ambushed? Had they spied Bedouin preparing to attack the boats?

There was no time for evasive maneuvers—even if they had known the problem—for the current suddenly sped up as they swept around a bend in the river. Then they heard it, a hoarse roar rising up like distant thunder, and they knew the reason for the warning shot.

They were approaching rapids.

A moment later, they glimpsed the picturesque and crumbling abutments of Jisr Semakh, the Semakh Bridge. The arches of the bridge still stood, though in degrees of decay, but fallen sections obstructed the course of the river. At only one point, on the left side, did the pent-up waters find a narrow breach, and there the furious water foamed like a floodgate between scattered masses of stone.

The shore party stood dismounted on the right, waiting to offer its assistance to the boats through the dangerous rapid, the only course past the ruined bridge. The crews beached the three boats, and the groups joined forces to unload the boats, lightening them for the ride through the rapids.

Sheikh 'Akil positioned himself atop one of the remaining bridge arches and pointed down to the channel with his spear. Around and above him, storks circled, squawking. As they approached the rapid, Lynch took the lead in the *Fanny Mason*, constructed of copper, making damage to it more easily reparable than to the iron *Skinner*. Having heard stories about the river from a guide who accompanied the Molyneux expedition, Lynch had already concluded that he might have to sacrifice one boat to save the others. If the *Fanny Mason* were "dashed to pieces, her fragments would serve to warn the others from the danger."[117] What Lynch failed to realize is that her fragments, if they didn't wash downriver, would be visible as a warning only too late.

All hands in the *Fanny Mason* paddled furiously, ready to jump overboard if necessary. Even with the sailors' best efforts and skill, the boat struck hard on a rock, throwing her sideways into the midst of the fall of water, threatening to capsize her.

At that very moment, though, the little wooden gig, *Uncle Sam*, topped the rapid, and as Lynch uncharitably wrote later, "The Arab crew of *Uncle Sam* unskillfully brought her within the influence of the current."[118] Thus, the little boat, with great speed, hit the *Fanny Mason* broadside, which oddly enough turned out to be her salvation. The *Fanny Mason* slid off the rock holding it in the waterfall and floated to safety. The crash damaged the gig, but its momentum put the *Fanny Mason* right, and both boats made it through the maelstrom. Then the *Skinner*, which floated higher in the water, dashed into the rapid and leapt the fall without damage, though one of the sailors, Hugh Read, fell overboard and narrowly escaped drowning. His shipmates dragged him back into the boat, dripping.

Gratefully, the sailors moored the boats overnight in a small cave on the west bank, almost obscured by the tall grass and weeds that sheltered the space from the force of the current. The shore caravan pitched its tents on a small mound that commanded a view of the river and the bridge. Lieutenant Dale busied himself with drawing the ruined bridge, which had two entire and six partial arches. Storks, disturbed from their nests in the reeds by all the activity, squawked overhead.

Examining the bridge on foot, Lynch decided that if his boat struck rocks in this, the flood season, the river must be very shallow in the summer. (He was correct.) His metal boats and companions had survived the challenges of the river well so far, with conditions much more advantageous than those that Molyneux faced in the dry season the previous August.

The expedition camped near the remains of Jisr Semakh, the ruined bridge across the Jordan River.

Molyneux's party had consisted of a much smaller contingent: three British seamen—Ian Grant, John Lyscomb, and George Winter—and his dragoman, Toby. They came equipped with the dragoman's two horses, a tent, canteen, and such stores that they could find on the British frigate HMS *Spartan*. The British vice consul contributed four camels. The *Spartan*'s captain, Thomas Symonds, provided Molyneux with a letter from the local pasha and another for the consul in Jerusalem, but neither Molyneux nor Captain Symonds attempted to gain the protection of a firman from the sultan in Istanbul.

The British expedition began its descent of the Jordan at dusk, rowing by moonlight. About fifteen minutes downriver, it landed its dinghy on the right bank in a little cove, only to discover a large Bedouin group camped just around the cove's head. While Molyneux and his men unloaded their belongings, a number of the Bedouin came running toward them. As Toby was some distance away with the camels, Molyneux greeted them with his loaded gun and with gestures indicating that he planned to stay just the night. He later learned that the group belonged to a tribe that had just lost a skirmish with the powerful Beni Sakhr tribe and had taken refuge on the west side of the river, instead of their accustomed lands on the east bank.

A natural boundary, the Ghor and the River Jordan marked the line between the Bedouin of the desert to the east and the farmers and villagers of the more fertile and well-watered lands to the west. Raiding and robbing were legal in mid-nineteenth-century Palestine and served as a primary source of income for the Bedouin as well as a symbolic display of strength.

Villages commonly paid protection money or tribute to the local Bedouin tribe to avoid being stripped of their valuables—or at least that was the prevailing impression to European observers. However, the reality of the Bedouin and farmer interaction was more complicated. Tribes and farmers intermarried to some degree and traded foodstuffs and livestock between them that created bonds that protected some villages from Bedouin attack—unless those bonds were violated.

Strangers passing through Bedouin territory, though, had no such protection. If they paid tribute to the tribe whose land they were traveling through, the Bedouin provided a guide who vouched for them and guaranteed their safety. If they did not pay, the Bedouin had no qualms about stripping travelers of everything of value—even their clothes.

Molyneux must have been ignorant of this custom. The next morning he found his camp surrounded by a group of some ninety men and boys—curious but seemingly friendly. Molyneux sent the boat across the river with some of his men and rode with the baggage himself to ensure that it made safe passage through the Bedouin tents. This particular group of Bedouin, perhaps weakened by their recent clash with the Beni Sakhr and intimidated by the British sailors' guns, did not demand tribute.

Molyneux's real trouble began when he reached the Semakh Bridge, which, as Lynch had surmised, scarcely had water in August to float even their small dinghy. The river split into small streams, each containing little water. After about an hour and a half of struggling along, followed by Bedouin from each of the several encampments they passed, Molyneux's sailors reached a point where they had to remove everything and portage the boat for one hundred yards or more over rocks and thorny bushes.

Then they reached a portion of the river with several weirs running across it, used to funnel water into irrigation ditches that watered patches of green that sustained the Bedouin flocks. The sailors sometimes had to pull down the mud walls of the weirs to float their boat farther downriver. The Bedouin—understandably but to Molyneux's annoyance—forced him to rebuild the damaged weirs "to avoid a row." His men often had to walk in the water, pushing the boat, which made it hard to keep their guns and ammunition dry and ready for use.

Around noon, just after Molyneux had shot at what he thought was a fox but his guide said was a boar, Toby, the dragoman, called out to him to load his pistols. He looked up and saw camels and muleteers "surrounded by a cluster of spears." Leaving his men also to load their weapons, Molyneux climbed the bank and saluted the dismounted sheikh, who stood before his camels and four mounted men. The sheikh explained that it was custom for travelers to pay when traveling through his land. Molyneux refused and showed the sheikh their weapons. In England, of course, he wouldn't have been able to traverse private land without permission, but Molyneux somehow didn't think the same arrangement extended to Bedouin territory.

After some yelling from both groups in incomprehensible Arabic and English, the Englishman led his camels and mules down to a ford, indicating to his men that his boat should come also. The sheikh and his men continued to argue. The sheikh asked for six hundred piastres for passage and said that his men would escort the sailors for two days' journey through his land. Molyneux offered one hundred piastres instead, which the sheikh treated as an insult. After more negotiating and a visit to a village where he learned that he was dealing with the Beni Sakhr tribe, Molyneux agreed to two hundred piastres. The governor of Tiberias, a friend to the British, heard of Molyneux's expedition, arrived, and, reading the pasha's letter, smoothed the way with the next sheikh down the valley.

As the expedition passed from one tribe's land to the next, it was repeatedly asked for more money, and Molyneux sometimes thought a tribe's land did not extend as far as the tribe pretended. At Seguia he refused to pay the amount the sheikh requested for an escort of four men, and the sheikh refused to send two. Thus, Molyneux decided to try it on his own, trusting the many gun barrels that he wore to protect him.

The next day, Toby and Molyneux rode ahead with the baggage, but the sailors and guides with the boat failed to make their rendezvous. After an anxious search, Molyneux learned that forty or fifty of the Messallieks tribe had thrown stones and fired into the water close to the boat. Wading into the water, the Bedouin pulled the boat to shore and robbed the men of their arms, ammunition, and everything else of value, as well as took the English sailors captive.

The Molyneux expedition to the Dead Sea didn't end at that point—but from that moment forward, it was doomed. Molyneux expended all his energy and resources searching for his men, spending a mere forty-four hours afloat in his leaky boat on the Dead Sea. Only upon his return to the *Spartan* did he reunite with his sailors, who had surfaced in Tiberias naked and starving. After writing a brief account of his experiences, Molyneux fell ill and died in November

1847, likely from complications of heatstroke from his time floating on the Dead Sea in summer heat.[119]

About a month later, Lynch, then in Gibraltar aboard the *Supply*, read a false account that Molyneux had been killed in a Bedouin attack, which strengthened Lynch's resolve to do everything in his power to make his expedition invulnerable.

How different had been the American expedition's experience with the Bedouin—at least so far. Lynch pronounced their camp on a small knoll by the ruined bridge to be "charming." Two American canvas tents stood with the boats' masts as tent poles, along with one Arab tent and one Egyptian (Dr. Anderson's)—all different colors. The dark, rich soil, due to the rainy season, was

> *luxuriantly clothed three feet deep with flowers. . . . The purple bloom of the thistle predominates, and the yellow of the marigold and pink oleander are occasionally relieved by the scarlet anemone . . . the Adonis or Pheasant's eye; the Briony, formerly used in medicine; the* Scabiosa Stellata, *in great luxuriance . . . and two kinds of clover.*[120]

That evening, the Bedouin took advantage of the sheikh of Semakh's unusual compulsion for his tract of land. He was required to entertain all travelers with supper and barley for their horses. Lynch decided not to avail himself of the privilege, but he enjoyed watching the Bedouin ford the stream in single file, galloping up the hill to Semakh for the traditional supper of a whole sheep and buckets of rice. The Bedouin returned late at night, making such a racket with their splashing and shouting at the ford that the Americans sprang to alert, grabbing their arms. They settled back to sleep, only to awake to the noise of Dr. Anderson's horse, which had become entangled in tent cords while trying to attack one of the Arab horses, "his bitter enemy."[121]

It was sleep they could have used. They didn't know it yet, but the next day the expedition was going to tackle the weirs that so tormented Molyneux and yet more rapids.

VI

More Rapids

The current ran at 2.5 knots that next morning, but it increased by degrees until at 8:30, Lynch and his party came upon foaming rapids that extended for three hundred yards through fishing weirs and the ruins of another bridge that clogged the riverbed. One of the men wrote that the stream promised dangers but few delights, yet a "true-born undaunted American never flinches from his duty." Indeed, he wished their adventure were a spectator sport, with one-half of Philadelphia, New York, and Boston to watch them tackle the rapids to come.[122]

Cultivated fields stretched from both sides of the river, indicating that the area was inhabited, but the sailors at first didn't see anyone. Lynch beached the boats before the first rapid, and the men unloaded everything. They tied a rope to a solid tree on the riverbank, with the other end managed by one or two in the boat. Fortunately, the water here ran ten to fifteen feet deep until it reached a ledge of rocks, so several sailors guided each boat by swimming alongside it until it reached the fall. They each shot down the rapid, one after another. The boats escaped damage, and no one was injured.

But five more falls lay ahead, and the river became shallower and more rapid. They opened a channel for the boats by removing large stones from a weir and eased the boats down with a grapnel. Then they found a sluice, intended for a ruined mill just below, which, thankfully, was wide enough for a boat to pass for some yards—until it grew too narrow. Again, the sailors removed everything from the boats, and, assisted by a few Arabs whom their presence had attracted, ported the boats down the rocky slope and launched them again in the river. They had to negotiate eighty more yards of swift and shallow water, studded with rocks, before reaching smooth water.

By that point, some two hundred Arabs from a village on a nearby hill came shouting down the slope and surrounded the men, who were resting on the riverbank after four hours in the water maneuvering the boats. For security, Lynch stationed one of the sailors at the blunderbuss installed on the bow of *Uncle Sam*, the wooden boat, though the villagers merely seemed curious at the odd sight of boats descending the river.

As the men boarded the boats and pushed off in the river, villagers caught hold of the sides and held on until the current—eight or nine knots strong at this point—loosened their holds.[123] The boats rounded an abrupt bend, one bank some sixty feet high, the other less so. Thick clusters of pink and white oleanders bloomed on both sides, and lily pads were fading in the water, as if past their season. One sailor killed an animal that Lynch described as having "the form of a lobster, the head of a mouse, and the tail of a dog: the Arabs call it *kelb el maya*, or water-dog."[124] It might have been a rock hyrax, which is common in the river valley, though not a water animal.[125]

In early afternoon, the lead boat, commanded by Lynch, caught and hung for a short time on a rock in a shoal rapid. He stopped to warn the other boats, so they could avoid the hazard. About two o'clock, Lynch spotted some of the shore caravan on a hill in the distance. Watching for the other boats, he spied spears above the top of the bank. Investigating, he found nine Bedouin resting on the grass, their horses tethered nearby. As he often did, Lynch initiated a friendly interaction by allowing the Bedouin to examine his watch. He stopped to make some remarks in his notebook, and the men began to ask for something that Lynch couldn't understand. When the Bedouin became insistent, Lynch moved away, climbing farther up the bank, where he spied the Bedouin's black camel-hair tent partially shielded by shrubbery. The land above the bank, about fifteen feet high, looked fertile but was uncultivated.

By five o'clock Lynch and his men had descended eleven rapids. In the last, one of the seamen, clinging to the boat, lost his grip and was nearly swept over the fall onto rocks. Only with difficulty did he make his way to shore. After the boats rounded a high bluff, the river began to widen again—until it reached sixty feet wide—with the current slowing to three knots. They floated past Abeidiyeh, a village of mud huts built on a hill on the west bank. Men, women, and children rushed down the hill, yelling, but the day was growing late, so Lynch continued on without stopping.

The water, eight feet deep here, became clearer, and the men glimpsed fish in the transparent water. Tamarisk and willow trees, with vines, crowded the banks. Ducks, storks, and other birds rose from the reeds, disturbed by the boats' passing. Beyond, several groves of wild pistachio grew. By eight o'clock that evening, it had become too dark to proceed, so the men hauled the boats onto the west bank by the falls and whirlpool of Bukah, an abandoned village. Some of them climbed up the steep slope to look for a place to site their camp. At the top, after climbing over stone walls and briar patches in the dark, they came upon the ruins of Delhemiyeh, another village, inhabited by Egyptians settled there by Ibrahim Pasha when he ruled Palestine in the 1830s. Now that the Egyptians were no longer in control, the Bedouin had repeatedly robbed the Egyptian fellahin (peasants or laborers) until they abandoned villages like these two.

Not long after, Lynch met a Bedouin on horseback sent to look for the boat party, learning that their camp lay about half a mile farther down the river, past the whirlpool. Lynch didn't want to chance the whirlpool and rapids in the dark, even with bright moonlight shining down on them, so he requested that some of 'Akil's men guard the boats, allowing the tired, wet, hungry sailors to bivouac for the night.

Lynch found the site sublime—with the wild whirlpool promising adventure for the morrow, its sheen silvery in the moonlight. High up on the banks, on either side of the river, lay abandoned and ruined villages. An owl whooped, its call reaching above the roar of the tumultuous waters. Late into the night one of 'Akil's men sang sadly to the sound of his rebabeh, an instrument shaped like a miniature spade, covered with sheepskin. As Lynch dozed, the Arab's song mingled with his dreams.[126]

None of the men had much in the way of dry clothing due to their repeated exertions in the water while handling the boats. One came down with dysentery that evening, which Lynch attributed to exposure or fatigue or both. The repeated soakings certainly didn't help, especially as a chill settled over the night, heavy with dew.

One officer and two men stood watch, two hours at a time, with the blunderbuss mounted and everyone else sleeping with a cartridge belt and their hands upon their fire-locks. In the morning, the expedition would enter the part of the river considered the most perilous because of the warlike Bedouin in that region. No matter how tired the men were from their exertions that day, vigilance was essential.

Wednesday, April 12—Limping a little from a sprain the day before, Lynch went out at daybreak to assess the whirlpool and the rapids. Their wooden boat, *Uncle Sam*, had foun-dered in the night, despite all efforts to patch her in the last few days. The beatings from the rocks during the previous day—which had only dented the metal boats—had broken the gig.

Lynch worried about the implications of the loss of the wooden boat. When they reached the Dead Sea, their shore party of Bedouin friends would no longer be able to trans-port their tents and equipment because there would not be enough food and water on the desolate shore to sustain them. Now, they wouldn't have the third boat to move their tents, food, and extra water from camp to camp on the Dead

Sea, hampering their explorations because they would have to return frequently to a base camp for shelter and supplies. However, Lynch now had conclusive proof of the superiority of the metal boats, which he would include in his reports.

On horseback, he rode south to where the Yarmouk River joined the Jordan from the east. There he spied the sharif riding toward him on his spirited mare, calling to some Bedouin creeping toward Lynch under cover of an overhanging bank. The sharif said nothing about the incident to Lynch but rode protectively by his side for the remainder of the distance. The Arab leader even helped Lynch choose some flowers for the expedition's collection, including one that had no English name, so far as Lynch knew. Its stalk rose seven feet high, each flower growing on a separate stem. Grass, flowers, oleanders, willows, and tamarisk, and on a sort of terrace farther from the river, oaks and cedar festooned the lush banks.

After they returned to camp, Lynch spoke with the sharif and sheikh, assuring them that he would pay for any damage to weirs or mill-dams that their passage might cause. However, he vowed not to pay for "protection" from local sheikhs or emirs, like one who had offered his services the day before. Lynch was treading on dangerous ground with that decision, for that was exactly what had landed Molyneux in trouble and led to the demise of his expedition. Wisely, the sharif and sheikh both counseled Lynch to give the emir a present because he had traveled some distance to greet them. Lynch presented him with one of the keffiyehs that the expedition had brought along for such occasions.

They set off downriver at 10:15. Lynch had reconnoitered the coming stretch of rapids, so he knew that, with high banks on either side, there was no chance of a portage around the falls, and the current was too strong for the grapnel. They had to shoot the eleven-foot rapids and hope for the best. In the middle of the channel lay a gap where the water burst out at about sixty degrees that would work—except there was a huge rock at the bottom, exactly in the channel. Not only did they have to shoot the rapid, but they also had to turn the boat at a sharp angle before reaching bottom. Moreover, that huge rock sat on the outer rim of the whirlpool that circled around and around into a sinking hole of foam. If the boats survived these ordeals, they faced two more fierce rapids within three hundred yards and then two more within a mile.

It was a daunting prospect, but all was not lost before they started. A large bush grew on the east bank, some five feet above the water. Lynch had one of the men go some distance upriver where the current wasn't as strong and swim across carrying a rope. The man tied it securely around the bush's roots. They couldn't be sure that the roots would hold, but they had no other safe alternative. Lynch didn't want to risk his own men, so he had four of 'Akil's followers swim by on each side of the *Fanny Mason*, guiding it. The men aimed the boat toward the narrow channel through the rapid. Then, tightening the rope, they let the boat tremble on the brink of the fall. Meanwhile, the sailors and several Arabs, stripped half naked, scrambled along the banks, gesturing wildly and clamoring to assist if any Arabs were thrown from the boat. The *Fanny Mason*—held tense in the apex of the current by the rope—swayed from side to side. When the boat's bow finally aimed in the correct direction, Lynch signaled for the men to let loose the rope. The boat plunged, leaped, and cleared the rock, floating into the pool below, while the Bedouin and sailors screamed to urge her on. Two of 'Akil's men lost their grip and swept through the rapids, rescued far below. The *Fanny Skinner*, under Richmond Aulick's direction, passed though the same process, with equal success.

When the *Fanny Mason* had cleared the series of rapids, Lynch sent the land caravan on to Jisr el Mejâmiá (Bridge of Place of Meeting), which, only three miles away by land, would be much farther away due to the winding of the river. The sharif and sheikh had advised that this would be the only place where the caravan could descend again to the river to make camp for the night.

Lynch allowed his crew to rest awhile from their exertions as they waited for the *Fanny Skinner* to catch up, and he took refuge under the shade of a blooming oleander bush. The heady fragrance scarcely compensated for the biting insects buzzing around him. He was so tired from all his efforts that he fell asleep anyway.

When the *Fanny Skinner* arrived, the boats pushed off again. Just after four o'clock they passed the mouth of the Yarmouk River, the Jordan's main tributary, some forty yards wide. Just before five o'clock, they reached another white-water rapid and beached the boats so that Lynch, on his hands and knees, could creep up the almost perpendicular two hundred-foot hillside to examine the path of the rapid. From the top of the bank, he ascertained that this rapid also required the men to lower the boats, one at a time, by rope.

It was almost six o'clock by the time the boats reached smooth water again, yet it was essential that they continue. Lynch had allowed the caravan to leave without unpacking sufficient arms, and the men on the river had only three pistols and one carbine among them. It wasn't safe to stay the night on the riverbank with so little firepower. They reached Jisr el Mejâmiá around 6:15—to find that they faced yet another fall and rapid created by the bridge that gracefully spanned the river with one large and three smaller pointed arches on the lower level, with six small arches above. Caravans traveling from Nablus to Damascus still used this bridge, beside which lay a ruined caravanserai, a walled structure where caravans rested after a day's journey, like missions built by the Spanish in the American West.

The river flowed under the main arch and then broke into two branches, the left side leaping down an eight-foot drop—only to smash into the rock face of the eastern bank. The shallow right branch flowed around an island and spread over a wide space, broken by rocks. To complicate the situation, twenty or thirty Bedouin tents occupied the eastern bank, with many women in black robes passing to and fro, preparing their evening meal.

Neither branch of the river made a good choice for a descent, but Lynch decided on the right branch because he dreaded sheer drops like the right branch offered. So the boats shot, one at a time, through the main arch and maneuvered around the rocks. They hauled the boats up on the bank, removed everything, and proceeded to the camp, a quarter mile below. On a small headland, the camp provided a good view of the bridge and the ruined caravanserai. With time to pause, breathe, and think, Lynch wondered about the name Mejâmiá, Arabic for "place of meeting." Could this be the "place of meeting" so named by Jacob because the angels of God met him there? They were still in Galilee, in the land of Issachar; opposite lay Gilead, the land of Gad.

The next night, Emir el Ghuzzhawy insisted that the sailors and Sheikh 'Akil and his men dine with him. At six o'clock some of the sailors set out to eat in the emir's black goat-hair tent; the rest remained to guard the camp. When the group arrived at the emir's encampment, a woman screamed out and wept upon seeing 'Akil. She recognized him as the murderer of her husband from a skirmish the year before. 'Akil showed no remorse, which Lynch interpreted as stoicism.

'Akil managed to keep a protective eye on the progress of the boats when no one else in the land party could. "We never tired of the company of this graceful savage," Lynch wrote, adding:

> *Altogether, he was the most perfect specimen of manhood we had seen. Looking at his fine face, almost effeminate in its regularity of feature, who would imagine he had been the stern leader of revolt, and that his laughing, careless eye had ever glanced from his stronghold on the hill upon the Pasha's troops in the plain, meditating slaughter in their ranks and booty from the routed Turk; or searched the ravines and the hill-sides, the wady and the valley, for the lurking fellahin and their herds?*[127]

Lynch may not have realized it, but 'Akil prospered because of a power vacuum. A Bedouin of the Hanabi tribe, the sheikh, like his father before him, had served various masters, including Ibrahim Pasha when he invaded Palestine.[128] After Britain and her allies forced the Egyptians out of Palestine, the Ottomans didn't have the resources to reestablish firm control of the region. In 1843, 'Akil had become chief of a group of irregulars in Northern Palestine. By 1847, he controlled Galilee from Haifa and Acre in the west to Tiberias in the east, with Nazareth in the center, and he would expand that power in the years to come. Some thought he might lead a confederacy of Arab tribes to throw off the yoke of the Ottomans. But former Arab leaders who were successful at that attempt, at least for a while, had grown sedentary with their established power base. 'Akil, for his part, never wanted to relinquish his transitory Bedouin lifestyle.[129]

"Why do you not settle down on some of the fertile lands in your district and no longer live on pillage?" Lynch asked him.

"Would you have me disgrace myself and till the ground like one of the fellahin?" he replied.

"Many of our most eminent men were tillers of the ground," Lynch said.

'Akil smiled.[130]

VII

Pilgrims by Torchlight

No longer did Lynch and his companions in the two boats allow the leisurely current—at least leisurely between sets of rapids—flow them down the Jordan, aided by a few oars to help the rudder keep them in the center channel. No, time was short on this day, Monday, April 17, and they pressed on in haste, aiming to meet the land party and camp at Jesus's baptism site for the night. In the late afternoon, they swept through another wild and dangerous rapid, almost a common occurrence now after so many. They stopped to sample the water of a small stream on the east side of the river, finding it clear and sweet. Lynch marked the temperature of the water at seventy-six degrees.

Suddenly a Bedouin thrashed through the thick bushes on the left, while more Bedouin shouted at them from a hill on the right. Alarmed, Lynch and his crew backed their oars and awaited the other boat to close, readying themselves for a skirmish. Then came a shot from above. Lynch assumed that the other boat had been fired upon.

"Shoot the first objects" you see in the bushes, he told his men.[131]

The lone Bedouin concealed himself, perhaps frightened by the Americans' excited voices or hearing their pistols cocked. Then the group of Bedouin disappeared. The second boat, the *Skinner*, rounded the bend behind them, and Lynch heard someone in the second boat shout that they had stopped for a moment to shoot at a bird—the sound of the shot. When the lone Bedouin reappeared after they had holstered their weapons, he explained that he was a messenger sent to lead the boat parties to their rendezvous with the land party.

Lynch and his men had nearly killed the greeting party's emissary.

Lynch took the Bedouin into his boat, learning that he was from a tribe near Jericho. The man brought their sheikh's present of oranges and cakes from Damascus. The sailors sampled both, and Lynch remarked that the oranges were especially welcome after the heat of the day. The cakes, though, were very good only "if you were very hungry" and "made-believe very hard."[132]

The land party, after leaving camp that morning, crossed Wadi Faria and came upon a young camel that had strayed from its owners. Grazing in the brown and stunted bushes of the ravine, it caught sight of the group on horseback and immediately dashed away in the awkward, yet rapid gait of its species. The animal was caught, and one of the Bedouin placed a hand on its neck. It immediately knelt down. Sheikh

'Akil mounted the prize without halter or bridle and sprinted away to put the animal through its paces. Upon their return, the sheikh's men put the animal to work as one of the expedition's beasts of burden.

At midday, the land caravan stopped for rest, the Arabs under colorful tents made from their abas, hung over spears, to shield them from the sun. In the mid-afternoon, they passed sections of a broad-paved stone road, probably Roman, then an abandoned village. They watered later in a clear, sweet-water creek in the Wadi Na-wa-'imeh. At the Ain el Hadj (Pilgrim's Fountain), in the plain of Gilgal, they encountered a group of Bedouin with long-barreled guns and powder-flasks made of ram's horn, which Dale thought might have been modeled after the ram's horns used by the Israelites to topple the walls of Jericho.

Meanwhile the boats continued as the sun went down. To Lynch, the river grew more unpredictable as the light lessened. Twice, they passed more rapids, treacherous in the darkness, though they hugged the boats close to one bank or the other. As night deepened, the heat of the desert day morphed into the cold of the desert night. The men pulling on the oars kept warm, but those sitting in the stern shivered.

The company had less than a quarter moon to light their way that night, as the moon was waning from the last full moon on April 8. The next full moon wouldn't occur until May 7. In near darkness, Lynch sometimes had the illusion that the boats were remaining stationary and the shores were flitting past; in reality, the river, with a tumultuous rush, was hurtling them forward faster than was safe. They couldn't tell if the next moment would "dash us upon a rock or plunge us down a cataract."[133] The Bedouin messenger was no help, for he, like other Bedouin whom they met, knew only the fords and camping places of the river, not the rapids.

It would have been prudent to wait until morning before continuing, but the group was wet and hungry, without dry clothing or food—both of which lay with the land party. But if they landed the boats for the night without their armed allies, they made themselves vulnerable. The names of the sharif or Sheikh 'Akil wouldn't deflect an attack without the leaders' presence. Nor did the boat party have the firepower of the larger and better-armed shore party. In the dark, they couldn't even effectively aim the blunderbuss, mounted in the bow of one of the boats.

Lynch decided to risk continuing into the night, determining that to pause until morning posed as great a danger as the rapids themselves in terms of vulnerability to attack or exposure resulting from such a cold, hungry, and sleepless night. Fortunately, he made the right decision, for they didn't encounter rapids that they could not handle in the faint light of the waning moon.

At 9:30 p.m., after fifteen hours in the boats, the company sighted the tents, long since pitched by the shore party. The location of the camp concerned Lynch, however, as soon as he learned that it lay on the bank of El Meshra, the ford in the Jordan River revered by Christian pilgrims as Jesus's baptismal spot. Lynch thought it a desecration to moor the boats at such a sacred spot, so they passed by and found a landing spot just to the south.

In the shore party, Lieutenant Dale, too, had objected to the pitching of the tents at that spot—but for a different reason. It occupied a place where Christian pilgrims approached the river for baptism, and Dale had feared that the pilgrims might overrun the camp. Already, a few groups of pilgrims had arrived, and their camps dotted the surrounding river-banks. However, the Bedouin of the land party had assured Dale that this wouldn't happen because the pilgrims wouldn't arrive until morning had well advanced. The expedition would have time to pack the tents and break camp before the pilgrims arrived.

Also, plane, willow, and tamarisk trees, with some agnus castus, acacia, and mad apple trees, crowded much of the bank, so Lynch conceded that the flat space the Bedouin had chosen was the best place for the tents at the ford. He still felt uneasy, but the boats had arrived so late, and the men were weary, so he decided not to move camp until morning.

As soon as he was able, Lynch bathed in what he, like other Christians, believed a sacred spot in the river. As he swam, he thanked God "first, for the precious favor of being permitted to visit such a spot; and secondly for His protecting care throughout our perilous passage." Then, he sat musing on the bank for a long time, his mind awed by the events that he believed had occurred in that very spot so long ago. He paraphrased Joshua 3:13, perhaps in that very place, "the waters stood and rose up upon an heap" as the host of the Israelites passed by.[134] Just a few yards away lay stones that might be the twelve placed in the bed of the stream to mark where the priests holding the Ark of the Covenant had stood.

That the spot had seen the baptism of Jesus himself befuddled Lynch's mind, for he believed that "the mind of man, trammeled by sin, cannot soar in contemplation of so sublime an event." Even the impetuous Jordan, on that glorious day, must have calmed and gently "laved the body of its Lord." He felt it almost a desecration for his mind to divert from contemplation of the sacred scene to the myriad cares that worried him, but he decided that "next to faith, surely the highest Christian obligation is the performance of duty."[135]

After a brief meal, Lynch posted sentries, and the rest of the party tried to sleep. The sound of a gunshot broke their rest during the night, causing them to spring from their tents. The Bedouin scouts had fired a warning shot and were shouting at one or more men across the river. When pilgrims were approaching, 'Akil explained, a number of Bedouin wandered about, hoping to rob Christians separated from their armed guards. The sentries thought they had seen thieves and were warning them off. The alarm had been false—but it demonstrated reassuringly that the sentries were keeping guard. At three o'clock in the morning, they raised another alarm. Stumbling from their tents, Lynch and the other sailors woke to the sight of "thousands of torchlights, with a dark mass beneath, moving rapidly over the hills."[136] The Americans struck their tents and moved their equipment and belongings three-quarters of a mile farther downriver, which they would learn wasn't far enough. Lynch sent the boats to the other side of the river with instructions to stand by in case any pilgrims were swept downstream.

Hardly had the sailors finished the move, when the pilgrims, mindless like fugitives from a battle, turned headlong toward the water. Some rode camels, horses, or mules among those on foot, all together a chaotic mob. The Bedouin guards stuck their spears before the tents and, mounting their horses, formed a barrier around them. "But for them we should have been run down, and most of our effects trampled upon, scattered and lost."[137]

But more were to come. The first group preceded the main body of pilgrims, who at five o'clock topped the hill in a "tumultuous and eager throng." In wild haste,

Christian pilgrims, mostly Greek Orthodox and Catholics, bathed in the waters of the River Jordan as a baptism ritual.

Copts and Russians, Poles, Armenians, Greeks and Syrians, from all parts of Asia, from Europe, from Africa and from far distant America, on they came; men, women and children, of every age and hue, and in every variety of costume; talking, screaming, shouting, in almost every known language under the sun. . . . Many of the women and children were suspended in baskets or confined in cages.[138]

The pilgrims hurried forward with a self-absorbed madness, heedless of obstacles or their companions. They stripped down to the long white gowns that they would someday wear as burial shrouds, rushed to the river, and threw themselves into the water. As the bemused sailors watched, each dipped himself or herself, or was dipped by another, three times below the surface in honor of the Trinity. They cut branches of nearby willow trees, dipped them in the water, and took them away as holy souvenirs.

As he watched the mad progression of the multitude, one of Lynch's sailors, later quoted anonymously in Montague's book about the expedition, wondered at the motivation of these thousands from eastern parts of the Christian world to come so far, exposing themselves to dangers by sea and on land, wealthy and poor alike, all for their fervent piety. Here was a whole family—young, middle aged, and old—on camels. Here a mule carried three children in panniers. There pack animals surrounded a group of acquaintances. Those not in the water lined the banks of the river, faces rapt, intent on experiencing the holiness of the landscape. "The poverty-stricken and the sumptuously dressed alike unceremoniously wash in the stream, while the countenances bespeak the happiness of their souls. . . . It is worth the whole voyage from New York."[139]

Some sailors wondered if the miraculous river had consecrated their two *Fannies* as it had the pilgrims. Not a single accident befell any of the thousands who bathed themselves in the stream.[140]

This frenzied baptism ritual didn't always receive such a favorable portrayal. According to an anonymous account printed in the 1848 anthology *Littell's Living Age*, the pilgrim camp looked like a "theatre of licentious revelry, and more resembled the ancient celebrations of the Grecian mysteries than an assembly of Christians." It was a Christianity foreign to the American observer, who explained the differences by saying that the group retained the traditions of their pagan ancestors. The account describes in detail how soldiers awakened the pilgrims before dawn for a march to the river lit by burning pine torches borne by soldiers posted at intervals among the multitudes, who also set fire to piles of dry thorny shrubs along the road. The fires cast a dazzling light on the dreary desert, highlighting the contrast of the verdant willows and grass of the riverbank. Pilgrim shouts mixed with the screams of hyenas, jackals, and other beasts of prey. By the time they reached the river just at daybreak, all had reached the fever pitch of fanaticism. The observer, perhaps affected by the frantic atmosphere, claimed that a thousand or more were in the water at once, most with little clothing and others naked, "thrusting themselves and each other under the muddy flood." Mothers plunged infants underwater until nearly drowned. The lame and blind forgot their handicaps and rushed at the water like young swimmers.

In the excited abandonment, the swift current caught one pilgrim and bore him down the river unto death. The struggles of the drowning man merited only a momentary glance from those surrounding him. Then the river claimed another victim, and then a third and a fourth. People made no attempt even to reclaim their friends' bodies, which disappeared into the distance, only, the observer imagined, to be swept to the desolate shores of the Dead Sea where wild beasts would devour them.[141]

In 1836, artist David Roberts, in a much less fevered account, confirmed that pilgrims caught by the river current sometimes drowned in the confusion. According to Roberts, a young Greek

> *struck boldly out into the current but in the space of a second was hurried into its vortex. He strove nobly to regain the shore, but the eddies caused by the rush of the immense body of water dragged him downwards; for a moment his hands were lifted from the water, and after a short struggle the lifeless body was hurried on to the waters of the Dead Sea. This happened in the sight of thousands, but so intense were they on their immersion that not the slightest attempt was made to save him.*[142]

By noon, the whole mass of pilgrims had finished their baptisms and disappeared as suddenly as they had arrived, headed toward the Jericho plains with an escort of Turkish soldiers. Only the perplexed Americans remained, like an audience after a magic lantern show, basking incredulously in the glow of the images they had seen. The thousands of pilgrims, dunking themselves in the swift stream seemed like a dream, leaving behind nothing but the trampled bank.[143]

Then the sailors took their turn, bathing themselves in the river solemnly, except a few who splashed around laughing. The expedition had required shielding from what Lynch would have thought would be a friendly group—Christian pilgrims—but Bedouin Muslims, "wild children of the desert," had protected them when the numbers of dazed holy seekers could have presented a real danger. Still, it had pleased Lynch to have met two Americans among the throng who had recognized the Stars and Stripes and the boat that, should it be needed, stood by to rescue any drowning pilgrim.[144]

Before leaving the baptismal site, Lynch oriented himself with respect to biblical history. They were on the west side of the Jordan, which meant the land of the Israelite tribe of Benjamin; across the river lay the land of Reuben. Not far away, on the west side, stood Jericho, the city with the walls that had fallen at the sound of Joshua's trumpet. On the east side, about fourteen miles away, the site of Heshbon, where Sihon, king of the Amorites, refused to let the Israelites pass. According to the Hebrew scriptures, Sihon and his people paid the price of death for their refusal. In biblical times, Lynch decided, the banks of the river must have been high and the water deep, or the prophet Elisha would not have required a miracle to recover the ax lost in the river.

Not long after the last of the pilgrims departed, a heavy cloud formed to the west, with a display of thunder and lightning before a rain shower. The storm, though, didn't prevent the Americans from launching their metal boats that afternoon for the last leg of the journey down the Jordan. Just after 2 p.m. they stopped to take on board Sheikh Helu of the Huteim tribe, who would give them safe passage through his lands. Then, as the river wound northwest to south-southwest, they stopped to fill their India-rubber water bags with fresh water—which would be in short supply once they reached the Dead Sea. The shore party, rather than shadowing the boats as it had been doing, instead set off in a direct line for Ain el Feshkah, the two parties' rendezvous point on the northwest shore of the Dead Sea.

Finally they neared the mysterious body of water that they believed had engulfed Sodom and Gomorrah. They had survived the rapids. No one had yet walked or ridden the distance from Tiberias to the Dead Sea. Molyneux and Costigan also had traversed the Jordan, but neither had researched the Dead Sea as Lynch and his men were about to do.[145] Though they had mounted the blunderbuss several times, drawing comfort from its ability to spread "fatal doses" in the interest of self-preservation, they had yet to suffer an attack—and they were almost there.[146]

Refusing to be distracted, Lynch painstakingly recorded the character of the river—the bank on the right of red clay, twenty-five feet high; left bank low, with willows, tamarisk, and high cane. The banks rose highest at bends in the river, he noted. The water ran twelve feet deep with a bottom of blue mud. A dead camel was floating in the river, probably caught in the current during the last storm. Another camel rested, exhausted, against the bank while its owner, despondent, waited for the animal to recover or die.

The river widened to fifty yards and measured eleven feet deep with a muddy bottom. The current was four knots. One sailor tested the water and found that, though discolored, it tasted sweet. Pigeons, herons, ducks, snipe, and other birds scattered as they passed. At three o'clock they began to smell the fetid odor of the Dead Sea from a small stream on the western shore, which they traced to the Wadi Hesbon. Though they couldn't see the sea itself yet, they spied the high, rugged mountains ringing it southward and westward.

About four o'clock one of the men sighted the sea to the south, over a flat, and then they were upon it. A heron flew by as the surface of the water ruffled, and they passed two small mud islands and a large one, some six to eight feet high, at the mouth of the river, which had widened to 180 yards and reduced to a depth of only three feet. Now the water smelled of bitters and salts—a nauseating mixture. Just as they reached the long-sought sea, a sudden northwest wind drove against the boats as though nature itself were forbidding them passage. They pressed on, undeterred, as the waves dashed furiously against the boats, crying "No admission."[147]

The American sailors weren't the first to associate the supernatural with the Dead Sea. In the fourth century AD, Saint Silvia led credence to the legend that the salt pillar of Lot's wife still stood near the sea. She didn't see it but believed the bishop of Segor, who said that it lay temporarily underwater due to floods. In the sixth century, the Targum of Jerusalem claimed that the salt pillar at Usdum embodied Lot's wife and that on the day of resurrection she would revert to human form. Bishop Arculf added to the legend that birds couldn't live near the sea or fly over it. Others claimed nothing could live in the salt-heavy waters.

Old Testament accounts describe fire and brimstone as the cause of the destruction of Sodom and Gomorrah, but since the Middle Ages, travelers speculated that the Cities of the Plain lay hidden under the waters of the Dead Sea. Henry Maundrell, who journeyed from Aleppo to Jerusalem in 1697, reported his frustration that he could not "discern any heaps of ruins" that would evidence "so dreadful an example of the divine vengeance." Unwilling to give up the idea of the flooded cities, he claimed that the procurator of

Jerusalem had told him that he had seen columns and ruins of buildings visible under the water of the lake. Maundrell supposed that an unusually high water level prevented him from seeing the ruins himself. Though Seetzen, walking around the sea in the winter of 1807, had seen no ruins, many devout Christians, including Lynch and his men, continued to debate the possibility.[148]

Coming of age during the fervent outpouring of the Second Great Awakening, Lynch felt God as an intimate presence. It's hard to imagine now, in today's more secular age, but in Lynch's devout Christian world, people took religion seriously. They prayed often and in public. They worried deeply about the state of their souls and the likelihood of being condemned to everlasting hell. They wrote about their reverence for God and fell to their knees when touched by the Holy Spirit. Believing in God allowed them to make sense of the universe—and the earthquakes, failed harvests, and destructive fires that came as punishments from God.[149] For Lynch and his men, the Dead Sea held overpowering religious significance, created, they believed, through the destruction of the depraved Cities of the Plain.

But now Lynch focused his full attention on the sudden gale pressing against them. He tried to steer north of west so as to make a true west course, because the river entry to the sea lay to the eastern side of the lake. He ordered one of the men to throw the log overboard to measure distance, but the wind continued to rise, so he had the man haul the log back in.

The Dead Sea waves were foaming brine, and the spray, evaporating, encrusted salt on the men's clothes and skin. Heavily laden, both boats moved sluggishly at first, the waves hitting the bows like sledgehammers. The salt prickled the men's skin and irritated their eyes. The waves generated by the storm already contradicted a widely held belief—namely that the Dead Sea was too heavy for the wind to create waves. Bartholomew Anglicus, a thirteenth-century Franciscan scholar, wrote that the Dead Sea "moveth not with the wind, for glue withstandeth wind and storms, by which glue all water is stint."[150] In 1662, Thomas Fuller aired an objection to the waves that decorated his map of the Dead Sea. "Would not it affright one to see a dead man walk?"[151]

But waves there were, and the boats failed to make forward progress, sliding rather to leeward, nearer the eastern shore. To lighten the boats, Lynch ordered some of the fresh water thrown overboard. Foolish perhaps, but he feared that the boats might flounder, and fresh water would have proved of no use to drowned men.

Was there something to the old Arab superstition that no one could sail on the sea and live? Costigan spent a few days on the water and was found dying upon the shore. Molyneux sailed for only about twenty hours and expired upon his return of a fever caught while upon the Dead Sea.

"It seemed as if the Dread Almighty frowned upon our efforts to navigate a sea, the creation of his wrath," Lynch reflected. Yet, he claimed he did not despair, though "the fretted mountains, sharp and incinerated, loomed terrific on either side, and salt and ashes mingled with its sands, and fetid sumptuous springs trickled down its ravines."[152]

Then, nearing six o'clock, the wind mysteriously stopped. The waters, weighted with their mineral content, also ceased moving. Within twenty minutes, they went from fighting a raging sea that threatened to swamp the boats to pulling oars rapidly over a "placid sheet of water" that hardly rippled.[153]

As they passed a small mud island, the sailors heard a pistol shot from the northern shore, west of the river's mouth. They adjusted their course toward the sound. A light breeze blew from the southeast, accompanied by huge white clouds over Judea, and, as the light faded, the sailors beheld their first sunset on the Dead Sea. The western edges of the clouds tinged with gold, then turned the color of roses, while all around them the rugged desert mountains changed from gray to pink to ghostly purple.

VIII

The Dead Sea

At twilight, with the sky reflecting the fading beauty of the golden sunset, the boats passed a gravelly point jutting out into the sea from the mud banks of the northern shore. Trying to discover their location before the light faded, Lynch sighted the narrow isthmus connecting the peninsula to the shore and decided that the land mass was the island at the mouth of the river that previous travelers had described— though they must have visited in flood years when the isthmus was an island.

He feared they would miss the appointed rendezvous with the land party. But what if their compatriots had been waylaid? Either case meant a wet and hungry night. The sheikh of Huteim, whom they had brought along as a guide, offered no help. He gestured his bewilderment, useless at determining their location; he was still frightened, from the gale winds that had threatened to swamp the boats, and disoriented, never having been afloat before. The shadow of the mountains obscured what little moon had yet to rise, so the men pulled at their oars by starlight, carefully trying to hug the shore without running aground.

At last, to the south, they caught the gleam of a fire upon the beach. Lynch ordered one of the men to shoot his gun to draw the Bedouin's attention and steered the boat toward the light. Shortly, however, the light faded, and the men had to rest on their oars, waiting for a signal, so as not to pass the spot in the dark. Then all became confused as they saw gun flashes and heard retorts and voices echoing from the cliffs, followed by more flashes and reports behind them from the shore they had already passed. Were their friends being attacked? How could they help? If they helped, how could they protect the boats? They pulled closer to land, parallel with the beach, sounding the depth as they went.

It wasn't until almost two hours after sunset that they came upon their camp at Ain el Feshkah, a brackish spring nestled beneath a towering cliff. The scouts and the caravan had become separated, and the two groups, trying to signal each other, while also responding to the signal from the boats, had caused the chaotic commotion of shots and shouts. "It was a wild scene upon an unknown and desolate coast—the mysterious sea, the shadowy mountains, the human voices among the cliffs, the vivid flashes and the loud reports reverberating along the shore," Lynch wrote.[154]

The spring lay about a mile from the lake, so they pulled the boats up on the beach below and left some of the Bedouin to guard them. The land party had pitched camp in a canebreak beside the spring, and the sailors, tired and wet, ate a hasty supper. The scene depressed Lynch, but he tried to get what rest he could in a "bed of dust, beside a fetid marsh" with "dark, fretted mountains behind and the sea, like a huge cauldron, before us, its surface shrouded in a lead-colored mist."[155]

As he lay there in the dust beside the sea, Lynch's mind would have drifted to thoughts of other nineteenth-century adventurers and scientists who had traveled to the Dead Sea before him, trying with varying degrees of success to ascertain the true nature of this strange body of water.

Ulrich Seetzen, who walked entirely around the Dead Sea in 1807, a six-day journey, was the first, traveling from Damascus and stopping at Kerak as he passed down the east side of the lake. He heard Bedouin rumors about ruins with the name "Bedra," which one sheikh claimed were so impressive that "he had to weep when he saw them."[156] Seetzen surmised these might be the legendary lost Petra, though he was unable to venture farther to investigate, as his companions from Hebron and Bethlehem, herding some sheep, newly purchased in Kerak, had negotiated with the Arab guides only to traverse the southern end of the sea on their way to Jerusalem.[157] It would be left to Burckhardt to be the first westerner to rediscover the rose-red city.

By observing driftwood deposited on the shores, Seetzen had discerned that the Dead Sea's level was not constant and he commented on the lack of life. He disbelieved many legends about the sea, such as that "iron swims upon it, and light bodies sink to the bottom—that birds, in their passage over it, fall dead into the sea, & etc."[158] However, he wrote in his journal that he found "no sea snails or mussels, only some common snails," which he collected on the banks.[159]

Christopher Costigan, an Irishman and the first nineteenth-century westerner to sail upon the lake, made the fatal error of making his journey in July and August when the Jordan River flows at its lowest level and the Dead Sea endures its most intense heat. Only twenty-five years old, he bought a boat in Beirut and with a Maltese servant transported his boat overland by camel to the Sea of Galilee, attempting to descend the Jordan only to abandon the effort due to the low water, transporting the boat the rest of the way, again, by camel. Little is known of Costigan's actual exploration because he died afterward from exposure, though John Lloyd Stephens tried to reconstruct Costigan's journey. According to Stephens, Costigan explored the entire lake in eight days, sounding its depths. He also claimed to have identified the site of the doomed city of Gomorrah.

Five other expeditions to the sea took place in the years 1837 to 1841, each carrying barometers and other equipment to measure the level of the Dead Sea.

The unlikely combination of George Henry Moore, an Irish aristocrat, and his companion, the mysterious William G. Beek, background unclear, arrived first, around the end of March 1837.[160] The Royal Geographical Society heralded their expedition with a brief but chatty mention in a report about recent research in geography: "We hear that a spirited young Irishman, Mr. George Moore, instead of loitering in fashionable pilgrimage along the beaten paths of Palestine, has actually devoted the past year to a minute geographic examination of the Dead Sea and its shores." Moore had been touring the East on a typical Grand Tour when something inspired him to abandon the well-worn haunts of a moneyed dilettante and engage in scientific exploration.[161]

Perhaps Moore met one of several Western travelers intrigued by the lack of scientific knowledge about the Dead Sea. The Reverend John D. Paxton, an American missionary, is a possible candidate. Paxton commented in a book based on his travels in the region:

> *Were someone, acquainted with navigating a small ves-sel, and capable of taking soundings and making a proper survey of the lake, to spend a month or two in doing it, and to publish a full account, with a correct map of the sea and the coast, he would confer a very great favor on the Christian world. It would be so easy of execution, and of so universal interest when done, that I wonder that none of those men who long for public fame have not before now thought of it.*[162]

Paxton himself had been influenced by Edward Robinson and Eli Smith, who had begun their work later published in the best-selling *Biblical Researches in Palestine, Mount Sinai, and Arabia Petraea*. Paxton met the pair in Jerusalem. They had deduced from their exploration of the region between the Dead Sea and the Red Sea that the Dead Sea lay below sea level. Appraising the landscape from the high ground above Aqaba, the port on the Red Sea, they noticed that the valley to the north "presents a much longer and greater descent" than the valley to the south, which indicated the difference in alti-tude of the two bodies of water.[163] If Paxton spoke with Moore and Beek, he might have shared the idea. The two might also have seized upon the notion that establishing the depth of the Dead Sea would, as Paxton said, launch their "public fame."

Moore and Beek's expedition lasted four months. They acquired a boat, two boatmen, a tent, and other stores in Beirut and sailed on March 15, 1837, to Jaffa in a hired coastal vessel. They journeyed from Jaffa to Jericho and then to the mouth of the Jordan River in the Dead Sea, where they set up camp and began taking measurements at the end of the month.

Their Arab escorts refused to cross the Jordan to the west side of the lake—necessary to bring them food, water, and other supplies—which hampered their plan to sail around it. Instead, they began exploring the eastern shore, including the Wadi Mojeb with its Arnon River that empties into the sea. Moore described the ravine as having red sandstone like Petra, though not as beautifully veined. While sketching, Moore saw ruins, which their Arab companions perhaps craftily "declared to be one of the guilty cities destroyed by the Almighty,"[164] but Moore judged they were recent remnants of a village.

When Moore and Beek began their depth soundings, it became clear they were amateurs at naval charting. They had neglected to bring tallow. Both the rope and weight for the sounding should have been smeared with tallow, so they could determine the nature of the sea floor by the materials that stuck to the rope and weight. Even worse, their rope was only 144 fathoms (267 meters or 864 feet) long—inadequate for some of the depths that they sounded, forcing them to buy more rope locally.[165]

However, they succeeded at what mattered: testing the altitude of the Dead Sea by measuring the temperature at which water boiled. Their technique sounds amateurish. "They boiled 'common rain water, collected from a natural reservoir in the rock,' in a tin which was intended for that purpose after a drawing in a pamphlet by a certain Colonel Sykes. The thermometer was inserted as nearly to the boiling point as possible, and the experiment was always repeated."[166] They based their procedure on methodology developed by Lieutenant Colonel William Henry Sykes, an Indian Army officer and naturalist. Noting that atmospheric pressure on water, which differs according to altitude, determines the boiling temperature, Sykes developed tables that corrected for differences in air pressure. In what today seems a more frivolous experiment, Moore also collected small fish from a fresh-water pool, which he immersed in Dead Sea water, confirming for Moore one legend of the Dead Sea—that no animal could live in its waters.[167]

A sheikh who had been assisting Moore brought news that Bedouin unrest had spread, and those accompanying the expedition refused to take them even to a nearby village. Moore traveled to Jerusalem to "see about all this," and, though he was able to make one more trip to the Dead Sea, he spent the next few months trying to obtain a firman that would grant the expedition safe passage around the Dead Sea so he could resume his measurements. He even traveled to Egypt to see Pasha Muhammad Ali himself and obtained a firman, but the governor in Jerusalem still wouldn't grant permission.

By November, Moore had returned to London, writing to his mother, "You will be astonished at receiving a letter from me at this address, and the surprise will not altogether be an agreeable one, when you learn that I have failed in an enterprise in which I had hoped to gain some little credit, which I pursued through so much toil, danger and mortification, and on which so much money has been expended."[168]

In addition to their experiments with boiling water that suggested that the Dead Sea indeed lay below sea level, Moore and Beek measured the width of the sea, and their sounding measured the depth at more than 300 fathoms. Other travelers, achieving much less, would have published scientific reports and a popular book. Moore did neither. Biographers speculate why, some citing evidence that Moore was in love with a married woman and spent time in the Middle East with her and her husband. The Dead Sea adventure may have aroused painful memories. Others conjecture that his mother and her friend Mrs. Maria Edgeworth, a published novelist, put excessive pressure on Moore. One afternoon, when the subject of publication came up again, Moore tossed all his diaries and letters, one at a time, into the fire, knowing that would silence the two women. Only two diaries escaped burning—one fortuitously of his time at the Dead Sea—and only because they sat in a box labeled "rubbish of all kinds."[169]

The second expedition, led by Gotthilf von Schubert of Munich, one of Germany's prominent natural historians, accompanied by two of his students and the artist Johann Bernatz, overlapped with Moore and Beek's expedition. Von Schubert expressed his surprise at finding a boat flying the British flag on the Dead Sea because no one seemed to be nearby: "We looked at the boat with profound empathy, and were already then happy because of the future [yield of scientific knowledge], which could justly be expected from this new, extraordinary sailing."[170]

Von Schubert's trip was extensive and his measurements many. Over 170 altitude measurements appeared in his book about the trip, including locations in Egypt, the Sinai, Palestine, and Lebanon. The Dead Sea, though, was a minor side trip, which von Schubert described as a "hurried ride" that lasted only a couple of hours. However, what his observations revealed surprised him—the Dead Sea indeed lay below sea level. "I should have suspected the level difference, because of observations of earlier travelers . . . but this possibility did not cross my mind!"[171]

Von Schubert, unlike Moore and Beek, had used barometers for his measurements. Though they left Germany with three barometers, by the time they reached the Dead Sea, only one was working, and the scientists questioned if it was "out of scale." They decided later that it had been accurate in measuring the Dead Sea as below sea level, but their questioning of the barometer at the time of the measurement prevented their colleagues from accepting their findings.[172]

A French count, Jules de Bertou, led the third group. De Bertou was already familiar with Moore and Beek's claim about the level of the Dead Sea, but he disputed their result because it contradicted his theory of the historical flow of the Jordan River into the Red Sea. He determined to duplicate the experiment conducted *"par un de mes amis*, M. G. Moore,"[173] and to verify Moore's results with a barometer. Upon completion of the task, he published his findings about the basin of the Dead Sea, namely, that it lay much lower than the Red Sea.

However, John Washington, secretary of the Royal Geographical Society, asserted that de Bertou's results complicated the issue. Washington's own measurement of the Dead Sea level differed from that of Moore and Beek, as well as von Schubert (though it still showed the Dead Sea below sea level), while de Bertou's measurement of Jerusalem corresponded to the other two groups.[174] Even worse, according to Washington, de Bertou's calculations showed "the difference between the Red Sea and the ocean was 630 feet. . . . Additionally, the elevation of the north end of the Dead Sea, according to de Bertou's calculation, was 1,340 feet below the level of the latter end, again, totally absurd, which made all of de Bertou's data very questionable."[175]

Joseph Russegger, an Austrian pioneer of mineralogical and geological research invited to the region by Pasha Muhammad Ali, took another set of measurements in the late autumn of 1838. Of the various scientists who journeyed to the Dead Sea during the competition to determine its level, Russegger probably had the best scientific education and certainly superior equipment. In addition to thermometers and barometers, he possessed exotic instruments such as aerometers, which measured the density and weight of liquid or gas; electrometers for measuring electricity in the air; and a magneto-galvanic apparatus that had large horseshoe-magnets.[176]

Russegger, too, spent a short time at the Dead Sea, though his measurements for its level appeared along with the most exhaustive list of levels in Palestine to date. Unfortunately, though, his comparison of the level of the Dead Sea against the Mediterranean differed from his comparison of the Dead Sea to the Red Sea, an impossibility. He corrected this error in later publications, but, like von Schubert and de Bertou, a question mark remained by his results in the minds of the scientific community.[177]

A group of English army officers in the Royal Sappers and Miners, in Palestine doing coastal surveys as part of the British expeditionary force that defeated Muhammad Ali at Acre, used triangulation—a different and at the time more accurate method of determining altitude. Lieutenant

John F. A. Symonds ran two triangulation survey lines. One extended from Acre to Tiberias, and another ran from Jaffa to Jerusalem and thence to the Dead Sea. Among his many computations, he determined that the Dead Sea lay below sea level. However, this observation, totally valid, was undermined by another. He had miscalculated the level of the Sea of Galilee.

The drama of all these attempts to prove that the Dead Sea lay below sea level and the reluctance of the scientific community to accept any even slightly flawed attempt as definitive played out in the pages of the *Journal of the Royal Geographical Society,* the organization that had first reported Moore and Beek's expedition in 1837. One of the primary movers in this not-so-behind-the-scenes maneuvering was Edward Robinson. His book, co-written with Eli Smith of Beirut, *Biblical Researches in Palestine, Mount Sinai, and Arabia Petraea,* stood in the nineteenth century as a cornerstone of the study of the Holy Land. The Royal Geographical Society awarded Robinson its Patrons Medal, and he maintained close connections with the society, appearing frequently in the pages of its journal.

Robinson wrote articles, including "Depression of the Dead Sea and of the Jordan Valley," which was published in the *Journal of the Royal Geographical Society*, that summarized and critiqued the measurements of the expeditions that investigated the level of the Dead Sea, and he would have shared his opinions with Lynch before the American expedition sailed. After describing the problems with each expedition in his article, Robinson concluded that a careful triangulation survey was required to settle the issue of whether the Dead Sea was or was not below sea level. He wrote that the survey "ought to be conducted in the same method and with all the

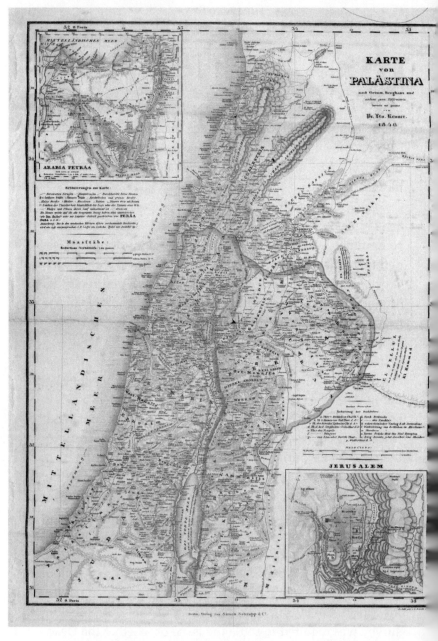

An 1840 map of Palestine drawn by Heinrich Berghaus, one of Berlin's leading cartographers, who created a series of influential maps of the region during Lynch's era, including a map of the Palestine journey made by Edward Robinson and Eli Smith to accompany their 1841 book. Lynch would have had access to this or another of Berghaus's maps. *Courtesy of the Eran Laor Collection, Hebrew University.*

caution and accuracy usually required in laying out the route of a canal or railway."[178]

Lynch would have known and agreed with Robinson's assertion that testing the level either by the boiling water method or with barometers of the day was unreliable, as demonstrated by the four previous expeditions. The level of the Dead Sea could only be definitively determined by another trigonometric measurement—that is, by physically laying out chains to measure distances upward and downward between the Dead Sea and the Mediterranean, which Lynch planned to do when they completed their observations and measurements.[179]

Hardly sleeping, Lynch noticed the moon rising above the eastern mountains around midnight. In the moon's silvery light, everything seemed haunted—mountains, sea, clouds—reflected eerily on the surface of the sea. The bell of Mar Saba, the Greek Orthodox monastery overlooking nearby Kidron Valley, pealed across the water, a Christian equivalent to the Muslim call to prayer. The sound, intended for wayfarers in the Dead Sea region, was welcome to Lynch's ears.

He dozed off, though, and awoke to rays of light, shooting up from behind the "dark and fretted mountains which form the eastern boundary of the sea."[180] He had intended to allow everyone to sleep late, so they could recover from the exertions of the day before. But shortly after dawn one of the Bedouin reported that the rising north wind had caused waves to crash into the boats, nearly filling them with water. The sailors, roused from not enough rest, hurried to the beach to retie the boats and dry out their contents.

Returning to the camp, Lynch described the nearby spring

in a clearing made in the cane-break, under a cliff upwards of a thousand feet high-old crumbling limestone and conglomerate of a dull ochre color. The fountain is a shallow and clear stream of water, at the temperature of 84°, which flows from a cane-break, near the base of the mountain. It is soft yet brackish, and there is no deposit of siliceous or cretaceous matter, but it has a strong smell of sulfur. A short distance from its source, it spreads over a considerable space, and its diagonal course to the sea is marked by a more vivid line of vegetation than that which surrounds it.[181]

The beach, between the cane-break and the sea, glinted with fragments of flint. In the water near the shore stood a number of what Lynch described as dead trees, though they were only approximately two inches in diameter. Lynch couldn't find the ruins that Edward Robinson had mentioned. Robinson had also reported that Bedouin had picked up pieces of sulfur as large as a walnut around Ain el Feshkah. Lynch saw no solid pieces of sulfur. There were, however, many pebbles of bituminous limestone like those Robinson described, which Robinson had believed testified to the volcanic nature of the region.[182]

Lynch found the desert surrounding the Dead Sea a region of "unmixed desolation."[183] The dimethyl sulfide rotten-egg smell of the stream tainted the air. Except for the cane-breaks and low, seemingly dead trees, no vegetation had matured at all, and the chemicals had turned the cane a tawny hue. The stark mountains, rocks tinged white with deposits of sea salt, and an unnatural sea lent a somber aspect to the area. Even the most arid desert should have a touch of genial nature, Lynch thought, but this place did not.

De Bertou had felt a similar sentiment:

> Here is desolation on the grandest scale, and beyond what the imagination of man could conceive: It must be seen—to describe it is impossible. In this striking and solemn waste, where nature is alike destitute of vegetation and inhabitants, man appears but an atom—all around is enveloped in the silence of death: not a bird, not even an insect, is seen![184]
>
> Such desolate hills would have brought to mind Jeremiah's prophecy: "Her cities are a desolation, a dry land, and a wilderness, a land wherein no man dwelleth, neither doth [any] son of man pass thereby."[185]

During the early part of the day, clouds partially obscured the sun. Later, the wind subsided, and the sun shone with unblinking brightness and intense heat upon the calm sea, appearing like molten lead or perhaps absinthe. The only upside was that there were no fleas, and the men's existing bites, which had smarted from the spray the day before, were healing.

Lynch released 'Akil and his followers, realizing they would not be able "to sustain their horses on the salt and acrid vegetation of this place,"[186] but to the American's surprise and pleasure, the skeikh revealed that he was on friendly terms with the Bedouin on the eastern shore of the lake. Lynch induced his guardian to arrange with the tribes to supply food and water for the expeditions. The expedition party would meet them at Kerak or on the nearby beach in

Heat causes a mist to rise from the barren Dead Sea shore.

ten days. The promise of sorely needed provisions was an amazing relief.

But not long after the agreement, Sheikh 'Akil revisited Lynch and asked to be released. Lynch determined that some of 'Akil's men had tried to discourage him from his commitment and offered to return the money that Lynch had advanced him for expenses. Lynch refused to release the man from his obligation, knowing the Arab would live up to the commitment because he would not break his word.

Lynch sent Sharif Hazzâ and his servant to Jerusalem to organize transportation of stores and to arrange for provisions from Hebron. Lynch also sent "everything we could dispense with—saddles, bridles, holsters, and all but a few articles of clothing." He also sent word to the pasha at

Jerusalem, asking for "a few soldiers, to guard the depot I intended forming at Ain Jidy [Ein Gedi], while we should be exploring the sea and its shores."[187]

That night the Bedouin held a feast to celebrate their departure. They filled a huge kettle with water and placed it on a fire made of wood that they had gathered on the beach. When the water boiled, they added flour and stirred the mixture with a piece of driftwood. When the mixture had the texture of paste, they took the vessel from the fire and added rancid butter. As Bedouin gathered around, scooping out the greasy mess, their bard sang into the night. Apparently it wasn't pleasant to hear—"the discordant croaking of the frog is music in comparison." In fact, Lynch thought an "occasional scream or yell would be absolute relief."[188]

At midnight, the bells of Mar Saba echoed again across the sea.

Thursday, April 20—The sailors awoke early to the sound of one of the Bedouin singing the Muslim call to prayer. According to Lynch, few answered the call.

A light breeze was blowing from the south, alleviating the morning temperature of eighty-two degrees. By mid-morning, Lynch was directing Dale and Aulick in the boats to start sounding depths, one boat heading straight across the sea and the other diagonally. The wind had died, and the sea resembled a mirror close to both shores, though the middle ruffled, as if there might be a current.

Toward evening, Lynch began to feel apprehensive about the boats and walked along the shore to the south to look, but he saw nothing of them. Along the way, he did catch sight of a beautiful butterfly, unable to catch it for their collection. As it grew dark, he directed fires to be lighted around the camp to serve as beacons for the boats.

Soon after dark, Bedouin from the Rashayideh tribe came to offer their services as guides along the western shore of the sea. Lynch described them as "the most meager, forlorn, and ragged creatures I had ever seen. The habiliments of Falstaff's recruits would have been a court costume compared to the attire of these attenuated wretches, whose swarthy skins, in all directions, peered forth through the filthy rags, which hung in shreds and patches, rather betraying than concealing their nudity."[189] Having a few of the Rashayideh as guides would have helped, but he feared their wretched poverty would prompt them to steal.

At eight o'clock, Lynch returned to the beach and thought he saw an object a long way away, but he couldn't be sure. The sea looked like a sheet of phosphorescent foam.

Finally, at 9:30, the *Fanny Mason* returned, followed at 10:45 by the *Fanny Skinner*. Increasing wind and heavy swells had delayed both ships. Aulick reported that the distance from the camp to the Arabian shore was seven nautical miles and the depth sounding was 696 feet. Dale, who made depth soundings diagonally across about every half mile, had discovered some kind of level plain occupying most of the sea bottom at a depth of 170 fathoms or 1,020 feet.

In the darkness the sea had rolled up dangerously, and the boats took in water, crests of the waves sloshing over their sides. Rowing and taking soundings simultaneously made for hard work—even before the pullback against the waves. The water was greasy to the touch, and, when the men's hands became wet while rowing, it produced a continual lather that caused their hands to smart and burn. When they returned to camp, their clothes were stiff with salt.

Sharif Hazzâ told the men that he understood that the Franks—a catchall term for westerners, deriving from the Frankish kingdoms of centuries past—behaved toward each other in an autocratic fashion, but it amazed even him that their country would have sent them to such a dangerous, desolate place.

IX

Deeper into the Sea

Fueled by their leader's determination, the God-fearing men sailed and rowed farther into the desolate wasteland of the Dead Sea. Europeans and most Bedouin thought the southern part of the sea a no-man's-land. Few reasons for travel there merited the dual risk of harsh climate and hostile tribes. "And verily this is a country that is deadly to the stranger, for its water is execrable; and he who should find that the Angel of Death delays for him, let him come here, for in all Islam I know not of any place to equal it in evil climate," wrote tenth-century Arab geographer Mukaddasi.[190]

Nowhere else in all of Palestine did the landscape so mirror the harshest teachings of the Old Testament. In this barren, salt-encrusted valley, God had destroyed Sodom and Gomorrah for their wickedness. When Lot's wife turned with regret for one last look at her home, God transformed her into a pillar of salt.

By now, some of the young men were wondering what exactly they had volunteered for—dreadful heat, hot wind, and supply shortages that could result in their deaths. Might there not be a curse on this godforsaken, lifeless lake?[191]

But to their commander and other explorers, the Dead Sea represented a place of supreme importance, worth any risk to investigate.

An ancient belief that persisted well into the middle of the nineteenth century assumed that the Jordan River once passed through what was now the Dead Sea. First, according to this legend, came heavenly fire, followed by the flooding of the plain, simultaneously destroying the cities and creating the sea. In an alternate but equally destructive scenario, God had caused a volcanic eruption, which would have resulted in fire and, conveniently, a seismic upheaval that created the depression where the lake then formed. Jean-Louis Burckhardt, in 1812 the first European to rediscover the fabled ruins of Petra, concluded that in biblical times "the Jordan once discharged itself into the Red Sea" until the great volcanic eruption destroyed Adma Zeboin, Sodom, and Gomorrah, and created the Dead Sea.[192] Lynch favored this theory.

Naturally, every religious traveler to the region looked for ruins of the destroyed cities, and their resulting books often included imagined sightings, though no proof.

If the American expedition discovered evidence that God really had destroyed Sodom and the other Cities of the Plain, such a discovery would serve as a terrible warning to the Judeo-Christian world to repent of its sins. For some Americans, this repentance went hand in hand with the

Second Coming of Christ. They deviated from the Puritan view that the Second Coming could not occur until all peoples of the world had converted. Instead, many believed that non-elect groups might be saved, including the Jews of Palestine. The expedition, then, bore a heavy religious responsibility and vast potential influence. These men could do what others had failed to do—prove the Bible as literal truth.[193]

Saturday, April 22—Around eight o'clock, the boats, heavily laden with provisions for several days, headed for Ein Gedi. A light wind from the southeast caused a swell that made the boats roll badly from side to side.

Less than half an hour later, they passed the Wadi Ta'amirah, the ravine that leads to Bethlehem. Robinson and Smith had described the head of the ravine as full of gardens, vineyards, and olive trees, with the aqueduct that fed the town winding around it.[194] Lynch fittingly remarked of the scene: "On one side is the sea, the record of God's wrath; on the other is the birthplace of the Redeemer of the world."[195]

At noon, the boats beached at Wadi Sudeir, the ravine below Ein Gedi, the oasis of Old Testament fame with its several springs and dramatic waterfall. Here vineyards produced wine for the kings of Israel, and King Saul searched for David in the wilderness nearby. Explorer John Lloyd Stephens even tried to determine which of the caves had served as David's refuge, though ultimately there were too many caves and no artifacts to associate with the story.[196]

The rugged surrounding cliffs were known as "the rocks of the wild goats" where David hid from King Saul.[197] Thus

Ein Gedi, one of the expedition's camps on the Dead Sea. When King David hid in Ein Gedi, associated with the Cities of the Plain in Hebrew scripture, "Saul took three thousand chosen men out of all Israel, and went to seek David and his men upon the rocks of the wild goats" (1 Samuel 24:2).

the spring had acquired the name Ein Gedi, Fountain of the Goat. Only the most patient of hunters ever spotted the wild goat of Palestine, the ibex. Its flesh is said to be savory—not that the Americans got a chance to sample any.

Lynch's men found the wadi dry, but the area around the springs flourished lushly with vegetation. There were no vineyards, but the Americans could see clearly from the remains of hill terraces that the oasis once had been an extensive agricultural center. Lynch wondered if analysis of soil samples they were collecting might indicate any special qualities that made it hospitable to vineyards. The men pitched their tents for their new base camp nearby and named it Camp Washington.

Lynch worried about his supply line. After he released 'Akil and his followers, the men depended upon supplies coming from Jerusalem or Hebron on camels or horseback. The current supply caravan, on its way from Jerusalem with Dr. Anderson and Sharif Hazzâ, might suffer an attack. If that happened, the expedition would be reduced to starvation rations.

As a backup measure, Lynch sent some of the remaining Bedouin to Hebron for flour. He would have sent either Dale or Aulick to Jerusalem, but he needed the officers to perform their scientific duties, including sounding the sea, taking astronomical measurements, and making topographical sketches. Their map was to be the first based on actual cartographic measurements. All previous maps derived solely from rough observation or the pacing off of distances.

By 1848, the technology existed to create a truly scientific map guided by instrument measurement, but that would have taken much longer than the three weeks the Americans were able to spend at the sea. They created their map of the Dead Sea, then, like many mid-nineteenth-century maps, at the intersection of observation, memory (in the form of previous maps), lore (from the Bedouin or other guides), and technology. According to Robinson, the locations of many wadis were well known, but some areas, such as the western coast from Ein Gedi to the southwestern limit of the sea had not been mapped even roughly.[198] If Lynch had brought maps created from past explorers' visual observations, such as those by Seetzen and Robinson, they would have helped with the general locations of major features, but he couldn't rely on them for precise distances or angles of terrain.

Dale and Aulick made 162 depth soundings that zigzag across the expedition's map in straight lines back and forth eight times. They used a chronometer and sextant to determine longitude and latitude. With a spirit level on a tripod, they were able to measure angles both in the horizontal and vertical planes—they judged changes in terrain such as the angle that a peninsula jutted out into the sea. Their training in topological drawing enabled them to fill in curves and gaps.[199]

In addition to mapping, Lynch also wanted to determine what previous expeditions had been unable to prove conclusively—that the Dead Sea lay below sea level. Lynch had his officers measure the altitude by boiling water, measuring temperature, and taking barometer readings.

Regrettably, one of the two mountain barometers—fragile yard-long mercury-filled glass siphon tubes inside brass housings—broke before the expedition completed its descent of the Jordan. But the other fortunately survived and would last until after they had departed the Dead Sea. Lynch took barometer readings every evening from the

Sea of Galilee, through the descent of the Jordan, to the Dead Sea and beyond. His barometer readings showed the Dead Sea at 1,234.589 feet below the Mediterranean. The barometers of that era weren't accurate even to the exact foot, however, much less to the thousandth of an inch. Comparing his records with more advanced measurements today, his barometer reading was off by about one hundred feet.[200]

Here at Ein Gedi, Lynch also began what Robinson and others had called for: a baseline for trigonometric measurement. Now the men would measure—using a chain for length and a theodolite for horizontal and vertical angles—up and down the hills and valleys until they reached the Mediterranean, so that they could compare the levels of the two bodies of water. In 1841, Lt. John Symonds, triangulating with a theodolite, carried two lines of levels from Jaffa to the Dead Sea and reached a calculation of approximately 1,311 feet below sea level—a good measurement unfortunately tainted because of Symonds's inaccurate measurement of the Sea of Galilee. Lynch planned to replicate Symonds's trigonometric measurement more accurately.

Easter Sunday morning began pleasantly. Respecting the holiday, Lynch put off any work that could wait until the following day, though, hammers and tools in hand, the men did make what repairs they could to the battered metal boats.

Nearly out of provisions, the idle sailors anxiously watched the craggy cliffs to the west for the sharif and Dr. Anderson to appear with a plodding supply train of horses and camels. Around noon, they saw them "creeping like

mites along the lofty crags descending to this deep chasm,"
and the pair, with their companions, finally reached the
camp by mid-afternoon with the eagerly awaited supplies.[201]

That night, the sailors visited Sharif Hazzâ's tent, and
some of the local Bedouin who had come to visit the sharif
danced for the Americans.

> *Ten or twelve of them were drawn up in a line, curved*
> *a little inwards, and one of them stood in front, with a*
> *naked sword. A mass of filthy rags, with black heads above*
> *and spindle legs below! Clapping their hands, and chant-*
> *ing a low, monotonous song, bowing and bending, and*
> *swinging their bodies from side to side, they followed the*
> *motions of the one in front. In a short time, one of them*
> *commenced chanting extempore, and the others repeated*
> *the words with monotonous cadence; he with the sword*
> *waving it to and fro in every direction, and keeping time*
> *and movement with the rest.*[202]

Their song referred to the Americans. "Lieutenant Dale
was strong and rode a horse well" and "The Kobtan [cap-
tain] made much work for Arabs, with his head."[203]

Ten years before, Robinson and Smith, on their trek along
the southern extremity of the Dead Sea, found themselves on
a cliff overlooking Ein Gedi and the sea from at least 1,500
feet above. The Dead Sea lay before them, its waters enclosed
on both sides by steep mountains, their bases sliding out of
the brackish water and then retreating upward, leaving only
a narrow band of shore below. The Bedouin called one of the
mountains slanting out from the western cliffs toward the
southeast Hajr Usdum—Stone of Sodom. Legend held that it
consisted of rock-salt too bitter even for cooking.[204]

As the two men gazed from their lofty perch, the waters of the sea looked "decidedly green, as if stagnant," though they did not notice this color when they descended to lake level. A slight ripple creased the water, and a line of what looked, from above, like froth edged it. It was a crust of salt. As they descended the cliff, Robinson and Smith noted an optical illusion, which had caused other travelers to say they saw islands in the sea. Near the opposite shore, they spied a long, dark-colored sand bank. A few minutes later, as they descended farther, they realized that it was a patch of smooth water surrounded by areas ruffled by a ripple. The eastern mountains, reflected in the still water, gave the "island" its dark green-brown color.[205]

Marauding Bedouin made the southern reaches of the Dead Sea much more dangerous in Lynch's day than they had been in 1838 when Robinson and Smith visited. Trying to mitigate the danger, Lynch had sent a messenger to the tribes along the southern part of the sea to obtain guides, but robbers had driven away the tribes, the messenger reported. A sheikh of the Ta'amirah tribe agreed to walk with his tribesmen along the coast, keeping the boats in sight, and to intercede with any Bedouin they might encounter. Even so, Sharif Hazzâ advised against making the trip—though to no avail. Lynch wasn't about to quit, leaving his tasks unfinished, after coming so far.

Lynch placed the sharif in charge of the camp, leaving one sailor on the sick list with him, and, for protection, the four Turkish soldiers who had arrived with the supply train. The boats headed south, keeping the Ta'amirah Bedouin on the beach in sight. They beached the boats for the night in a little cove just north of Wadi Mubughghik, a ravine with walls one thousand feet high. It was five miles or so from

A. TA'ÂMIRAH.

Marauding Bedouin made the southern reaches of the Dead Sea dangerous to traverse. Summoned by a messenger, a sheikh of the Ta'amirah tribe agreed to keep the boats in sight and to intercede with any other Bedouin that the expedition might encounter.

Usdum, the salt mountain that dominated the landscape to the south.

Since the loss of the wooden dinghy, *Uncle Sam*, they couldn't transport the tents, so from the boats the sailors removed the awnings they used as sunshades and rigged them as shelters for the night. A hot wind from the northwest began about 8:30 p.m. and raised the temperature from eighty-two to eighty-six degrees over the next half hour. It was the expedition's introduction to the sirocco, the hot, dust-laden wind from the deep desert. It made the space under the awnings so oppressively hot that the men couldn't endure even a handkerchief to protect their faces from the wind. They crawled out under the stars, with their feet near the water, and tried to sleep, as Lynch put it, "*à la belle etoile.*"[206] Fearing ambush, they slept in their clothes, guns at hand.

Lynch didn't sleep much, noting the meteors that fell overhead toward the north. The wind finally abated toward dawn, and the thermometer fell to seventy-nine degrees. "Notwithstanding the oppressive heat, there was a pleasure in our strange sensations, lying in the open air, upon the pebbly beach of this desolate and unknown sea, perhaps near the sites of Sodom and Gomorrah; the salt mountain of Usdum in close proximity, and nothing but bright, familiar stars above us."[207]

Lynch awoke before sunrise with a young quail at his side where it had nestled during the night for shelter from the sirocco. The sailors set off in variable wind about 5:30 a.m. directly toward the north point of Usdum, called Rash Hish, Cape Thicket, still hugging the shore, with the Ta'amirah tribesmen in sight. The boats coasted southward while the officers sketched the topography. The cliff face from the night before decreased until it ended in the salt mountain Usdum.

Lynch set one of the men to sound frequently for the ford that Seetzen, Robinson, and others mentioned as lying near the southern end of the sea. The depth of the water decreased and increased a few times, so they might have passed a ford, though they couldn't be sure. They didn't see the line of foam that Molyneux mentioned. About eight o'clock in the morning, they came alongside Muhariwat ("the Surrounded"), a ravine with lush vegetation from a spring, interspersed with gravel and sand, which lengthened toward Usdum.

Usdum, Sodom. The very name evoked intense associations. Here Lynch quoted Roman historian Josephus on the infamous pillar of salt. "I have seen it, and it remains at this day."[208]

Usdum stood in isolated splendor against the blue of the Dead Sea, though it didn't look like a mass of salt to Lynch. Nor did it look much like a pillar that could have been Lot's wife. Perhaps calcium carbonate coated the mass, which some mistook for salt. When the boats landed on the Usdum peninsula, a flat, marshy delta, the soil, encrusted with salt and bitumen, yielded to Lynch's footstep.

Half an hour later, they pushed off and steered east-southeast, sounding as they went. At nine o'clock on the eastern shore, they saw it—a "lofty, round pillar," detached from the mass of Usdum by a deep but narrow chasm. Bedouin had confirmed the pillar's existence, but until now Lynch hadn't known whether to believe that it existed.

Immediately, they pulled toward the shore, the boats running aground in the shallow waters two hundred feet from the shoreline. Lynch and Anderson climbed out of the boat to take samples of the pillar. So soft was the soil that their feet sank into the beach. They found the pillar

*to be of solid salt, capped with carbonate of lime, cylindrical
in front and pyramidal behind. The upper or rounded part
is about forty feet high, resting on a kind of oval pedestal,
from forty to sixty feet above the level of the sea. It slightly
decreases in size upwards, crumbles at the top, and is one
entire mass of crystallization. A prop, or buttress, connects
it with the mountain behind, and the whole is covered with
debris of a light stone color. Its peculiar shape is doubtless
attributable to the action of the winter rains.*[209]

They had come to prove the Hebrew scriptures, and yet
they were explaining the topography in terms of natural,
rather than divine, phenomena. Still, the men joked that the
formation must have been Lot's wife.[210]

The shallowness of the water at the south end of the
sea frustrated their efforts to take a meridian observation
to mark the lake's extremity. The *Fanny Mason* ran aground
in six inches of water. The *Fanny Skinner*, with her lighter
weight, got a little closer, but she hit bottom about three hundred yards from the beach. Lieutenant Dale climbed into the
water, planning to wade to shore, but his feet sank through
repeating layers of slimy mud and crusty salt, before he
reached firm footing. Presumably, he removed his boots, for
when he finally did reach the beach, the sand was so hot that
it burned his feet.

Continuing inland for another hundred yards, Dale
faced more complications. Due to the angle of the sun, the
men were unable to shoot it with a sextant to determine
their latitude. They would have to rely on measuring the
North Star that night. As Dale returned to the boat, one of
the sailors attempted to carry him, thus sparing him the
indignity of having to wade through mud and salt again.

The Pillar of Salt at Usdum, which many believed to be the remains of Lot's wife, whom God transformed for looking back with regret upon her home among the Cities of the Plain.

That arrangement, though wonderfully gallant, resulted in the comic sight of the two sinking ever farther into the briny muck. They wisely separated and slogged through the hot mess. At points where the surface held firm—or at least firmer—they tried to make a run for it, which they described as dashing "over burning ashes," perspiration flowing from every pore.[211] When they finally reached water, even the salt-laden eighty-eight-degree wetness was welcome.

All hands back in the boats now, they ghosted along in the shallow water toward the lush, though marshy outlet of the spring at Wadi es Safieh ("clear ravine"). The water here ran shallow and motionless, reflecting the sunlight, so the sailors had trouble distinguishing water from land. On the shore they noted pieces of driftwood, encrusted with salt. As the thermometer registered ninety-five degrees, there was no shade except what the awnings meagerly offered. The glare was blinding, and the heat became so intense that even breathing proved difficult.

On one side of the sea lay the salt mountain of Usdum, rugged and worn, its white pillar reminding all of God's destruction of the Cities of the Plain. The barren cliffs of Moab, with its caves that once gave Lot shelter, occupied the other side of the sea. The ruins of the sinful cities Sodom and Gomorrah lay underwater just to the north of these landmarks, Lynch decided.

The depressing setting brought to mind the two previous sailors who died as a result of their audacity in attempting to explore such an inhospitable body of water. The northern extremity of Usdum, Lynch named Point Costigan and the southern end Point Molyneux in tribute to them.

They turned the boats northeast, away from the desolate southern shore. It was mid-afternoon now, and nimbus clouds in the east threatened a storm. By 3:30 the wind had ceased, though, and the temperature had risen to an oppressively hot ninety-seven degrees. A transparent purple haze hung over the mountains, moment by moment growing ever darker and more ominous.

Then a "blistering hurricane" struck from the southeast, which threatened to drive the boats out to sea, away from what shelter the shore could offer.[212] An explosive gust rocked the boats so hard that it felt like an earthquake. The men hurriedly took in the sails, then pulled as hard on the oars as they could, aiming for shore. For a few moments, it seemed as though the wind might drive them out to sea, where the waves increased with the wind and would swamp the boats. The temperature continued rising, now 102 degrees, the hot wind gusting and rocking the boats mercilessly. The sailors closed their eyes against the fiery sting of wind and salt water, still rowing as hard as they could. Lynch, though, had to steer, so he couldn't close his eyes. The intense heat blistered his eyelids.

They took refuge—at least from the threatening onslaught of the waves—by landing at Wadi Humeir, a ravine near the southernmost part of the Dead Sea. Some of the men headed up the ravine, searching for a spot free of the stifling wind. Others ran a few yards from one of the boats, only to be driven back by the intense glare, and returned to crouch under the awnings. One of the men considered himself fortunate to have spectacles to protect his eyes—but soon found that their metal frames became so hot that he had to remove them. The buttons of their coats burned to the touch. Desperate, they set up a bivouac on the dry marsh of the wadi, among some dead bushes.

Walking farther up the ravine, they searched for water to relieve their torment. Rather than a stream, they located two pools sufficiently fresh to contain minnows and to be surrounded by a few succulent plants and ferns. The men gratefully bathed in the pools, but their relief lasted only a moment. As soon as their skin left the cool protection of the water, the moisture evaporated, leaving their skin parched. Nothing except the minnows moved, though the hot wind moaned through the ravine and the withered branches of a palm tree. Any life, even insects, had long since sought shelter under rocks or in another wadi better protected from the wind.

Curious, Lynch returned to where he could view the sea. A mist, purple on this eastern side and yellow on the western, curtained the wind, now a tempest. The sun, blazing red among bronzed clouds, appeared as though covered in smoked glass. "Thus may the heavens have appeared just before the Almighty in his wrath rained down fire upon the Cities of the Plain," Lynch thought.[213]

Then, surprisingly, smoke rose from the peninsula, now to the north. Was this evidence of friend or foe? The Ta'amirah tribesman who accompanied them pointed out the smoke, terrified, and Lynch could do nothing to persuade him to take a message to whatever Bedouin group it might be. Instead, the tribesman squatted down a few yards from the sailors, shaking his head and murmuring fearfully that they would be attacked in the night. But the Bedouin never attacked unless they had an advantage, and, wrote Lynch, "Fifteen well-armed Franks can, in that region, bid defiance to anything but surprise."[214] As long as they were vigilant, and they would be, a surprise wasn't likely.

They might not face a human attack, but the sky grew angrier as the day passed into evening. Again, defying all expectations, the temperature increased as night approached.

By eight o'clock that evening, the temperature had soared to 106 degrees at a measurement of five feet above the ground (and two degrees fewer four feet lower). Desperate for the respite of that slight difference, the men threw themselves downward on top of cracked earth and dry or dead vegetation. A couple of enterprising men tried to use an awning to break the wind that felt more like a furnace than natural air, but the brutal rush threw it over instantly.

Nor did drinking water quench their thirst, for, even though they didn't feel themselves perspire, any liquid seemed to dissipate as they drank it. By nine o'clock their water containers lay empty. They tried to sleep, but, if anyone did, he dreamed of cool beverages poured down his parched throat. Only mosquitoes stirred, seemingly immune to the hellish temperature, and their stings tormented the men relentlessly.

Still, they couldn't let down their guard. As it grew darker, they could hear shouts and see more clearly the gleam of fires at a Bedouin encampment through the thicket to their right. By turns, the sailors kept watch. "Those who have never felt thirst, never suffered in a Simoom in the wilderness, or been far off at sea, with 'water, water everywhere, nor any drop to drink' can form no idea of our sensations," Lynch observed.[215]

Only the inhabitants of Dante's *Inferno* could understand their torment.

X

Challenges Continue

The sailors on guard as sentries forced themselves upright. The rest of the men lay on the ground, stunned by intense heat and swirling dust. In and out of feverish sleep, they craved cool drops of water, chastising themselves for moments when they had wasted it in the past, not realizing that it was more precious than pearls.

The tribesman with them had not slept at all, Lynch discovered when he went out to check on the sentries. The poor man was still squatting in the same position as before, his gaze fixed with fear on the Bedouin fires to the north.

The temperature began to diminish. By midnight, it had dropped to ninety-eight degrees, and the wind had shifted to the north, lessening its fervor. The temperature continued

to fall until by four o'clock in the morning it reached a relatively cool eighty-two degrees.

At daybreak, signs of life emerged after the storm. A black bird floated across the sky. Then a flock of birds crossed the shore. Storks noiselessly joined them. Lynch stood, stretching his cramped muscles and went to the wadi to bathe. But before he reached the water, he heard voices in the cliffs above, and then a gunshot echoed from the ravine. Lieutenant Dale and Midshipman Aulick ran to Lynch's side.

Some of the sailors were filling water bottles at the spring when they heard the shot. They noticed several Bedouin women just to the north of their camp. The women allowed Mustafa, the interpreter-cook, to draw near enough to speak, but when he moved closer, they retreated. The women asked him who the Americans were and why they had come to this place. Mustafa explained, but the women still didn't understand why strangers would visit such an inhospitable location.

About an hour later, a sheikh approached the camp, followed by some thirty or so Bedouin armed with a motley assortment of old guns, lances, clubs, and tree branches. The men were singing. Not sure whether the song was a peaceful gesture or a kind of war cry, Lynch gathered his men, each with his weapon, planted an American flag, loaded the blunderbuss, and "drew a line upon the ground."[216] Through Mustafa, Lynch told the Bedouin that if they passed the line the Americans would fire. Immediately, the Arabs squatted down, a non-threatening movement indicating that they wanted to parley.

The Bedouin explained they were of the Ghaurariyeh tribe, and they begged for alms. Lynch surmised that, if his troops were not so well armed, the Bedouin would have demanded rather than asked. The men were weak from hunger, though, so Lynch gave them some food. Because they had no water pipe to share, Lynch also gave them tobacco, asking them to take a letter to Sheikh 'Akil in Kerak about their planned rendezvous, paying them a few coins to do so.

These Bedouin, confused, had never seen a boat before. How did the boats not sink when all the sailors took their seats? How could the boats possibly cross the water without legs? Mustafa told them to wait awhile, and they would see the oars do the work of legs. With the formalities of tobacco and conversation satisfied, the sailors stowed the spring water in the boats. The Bedouin helped them push off the beach and continued to watch until the boats disappeared from sight.

The next day, after a meager breakfast—a small cup of coffee each—they set off toward their base camp at Ein Gedi to replenish their supplies.

The wind, sun, and water conditions together created a marvelous refraction of the atmosphere. Lynch watched from the *Fanny Mason* as the *Fanny Skinner* rounded a point, and the boat seemed to levitate above the water. Her entire structure, from the waterline upward was clearly visible, though the spit of land should have obscured much of it. For a moment the men wondered if the elements had degraded their faculties and they were hallucinating.

Lynch had begun to worry about their health, as well as their mental state, as he was ultimately responsible for bringing them into such a noxious environment. Despite a high wind and waves, all the men appeared drowsy, all in his boat asleep except for those who rowed . . . with half-closed eyes. Lynch kept himself awake because he had to steer and record observations for the official record of the journey. This nearly irresistible stupor fell hardest in the heat of the day, but it never really disappeared even when the sun's glare faded and the temperature fell in the evening. Its effect must be cumulative, he decided, worsening the longer they stayed in this harsh environment; it made even small chores, such as two hours' sentry duty, seem twice as long.

Each man's body appeared bloated. "The lean had become stout, and the stout almost corpulent; the pale faces had become florid, and those which were florid, ruddy."[217] Even small scratches festered because of the salt water, so most had developed many small pustules. "The men complained bitterly of the irritation of their sores, whenever the acrid water of the sea touched them. Still, all had good appetites, and I hoped for the best."[218]

Most nineteenth-century westerners believed that the air itself, particularly putrid air, could carry contagion—hence the etymology of malaria, from *mala aria* in medieval Italian, literally: bad air. But there was so little in the way of flora or fauna to decompose and contaminate the air. The fetid odor around the sulfurous thermal springs continued to worry them, yes, and, true, they had collected three birds floating dead on the sea—but surely the birds had died from exhaustion trying to fly the long distance across the water. By the 1840s, microscopes were revealing germs swimming in water, but scientists hadn't yet realized the connection between those germs and disease.

One of the Ta'amirah tribesmen told Lynch about how Ibrahim Pasha, during the period he ruled Palestine, tried

to settle three thousand Egyptians on the shore of the Dead
Sea, which led ultimately to their deaths. Surely these numbers were exaggerated, though. Bad air around the Dead Sea
itself couldn't have caused that many deaths. Thousands of
Egyptian settlers and deserters remained in Palestine after
the Egyptian retreat in the early 1840s. Many had died of disease and Bedouin harassment.[219] But Lynch was wrong that
the region contained no contagion. The mosquitoes that bred
in swampy areas and harassed the men in the heat meant
that malaria—the bad air itself—was endemic in Palestine.
Another half century would pass before anyone knew that
mosquitoes carried the illness.[220]

As they rowed toward Camp Washington, the sea, unstirred
by any breeze, lay smooth, somber, and gray, like a "vast cauldron of metal, fused but motionless."[221] Water evaporated into a
transparent but purple-tinged vapor, giving, in the distance, the
appearance of smoke rising from burning sulfur.

At 1:30 p.m., the men spotted the white tents of their
camp at Ein Gedi and the distinctive line of vegetation
that promised water, shade, and rest. A camel was lying on
the beach near two Bedouin who, seeing the boats, came
toward them shouting and gesturing incomprehensibly.
More gratifying, though, came the sharif's obvious delight
at their safe return.

However, their pleasure at reaching Ein Gedi diminished
when Lynch read a letter that had arrived from the consul in
Jerusalem, the first word they had received from the outside
world since reaching the sea. In the weeks they had spent in
Palestine, the rest of the world had ceased to seem real, as
if all that existed now were the inhospitable and cursed sea
and the Bedouin who sometimes threatened and sometimes
befriended.

Jasper Chasseaud's letter intruded upon this strange place, reminding them that a world outside existed. The letter announced the death of former president John Quincy Adams, who years before had rushed the completion of the *Brandywine* to transport the Marquis de Lafayette back to France, accompanied by Lynch and Maury. It seemed a lifetime ago, and the news distressed the men of the expedition, but, Lynch decided, the "thought of death harmonized with the atmosphere and the scenery" of desolation and decay. They lowered the Stars and Stripes to half-mast, and the next day they fired a twenty-one-gun salute. "The reports reverberated loudly and strangely amid the cavernous recesses of those lofty and barren mountains."[222]

Chasseaud also relayed information about the fire of revolutions that were sweeping Europe, attempting to upset the conservative order dictated by the Congress of Vienna after Napoleon's final defeat. Lynch, ever the democrat, foretold, despite the uprisings about which he read, that the time was coming when the "whole worthless tribe of kings" would be swept away.[223]

That evening, the men climbed up the wadi over debris washed down by seasons of winter rains, toward the spring. A short distance up the ravine, they surprisingly discovered evidence of human habitation. They had observed other caves with hand-hewn markings before, but these displayed impressive craftsmanship, with arched openings and limestone sills. The Bedouin told them that these caves dated "from time immemorial."[224]

Some years before, the Bedouin claimed, one of their tribe had climbed into one of the arched openings and found the original caves enlarged into enormous chambers. But the cave entrances were cut perpendicular into the rock, some distance up from ground level, and the sailors could see no path ascending to them. For a moment, they considered contriving some way up to them, but the heat of the day discouraged their intentions for such unplanned exertion. The shade of the ravine overhang plus the cool spring water promised by the tamarisk, oleander, and cane trees proved simply too inviting.

> *Far in among the cane, embowered, imbedded, hidden deep in the shadow of the purple rocks and the soft green gloom of luxuriant vegetation, lapsing with a gentle murmur from basin to basin, over the rocks, under the rocks, by the rocks, and clasping the rocks with its crystal arms, was this little fountain-wonder. The thorny* nubk *and the pliant* osher *were on the bank above; yet lower, the oleander and the tamarisk; while upon its brink the lofty cane, bent by the weight of its fringe-like tassels, formed bowers over the stream fit for the haunts of Naiads. Diana herself could not have desired a more secluded bath than each of us took in a separate basin.*[225]

After bathing, they returned refreshed to the camp where they enjoyed the sugar and lemons, brought by the messenger, in the form of lemonade and coffee. Sheltered from the hot sun, with a breeze flowing through the tent, they enjoyed the moment.

> *This place, which at first seemed so dreary, had now become almost a paradise by contrast. The breeze blew freshly, but it was so welcome a guest, after the torrid atmosphere of noon, that we even let it tear up the tent stakes, and knock the whole apparatus about our ears, with*

a kind of indulgent fondness, rather disposed to see some-thing amusing in the flutter among the half-dried linen on the thorn-bushes. This reckless disregard of our personal property bore ample testimony to our welcome greeting of the wind.[226]

Some of the Ta'amirah Bedouin, taking advantage of the Americans' protection, harvested their scanty patches of barley nearby. They used their swords to cut the grain. Then, to thresh it, they threw it on a circular, hard-trampled plot of ground, around which, going in circles, went three donkeys, abreast, that, unmuzzled, grabbed mouthfuls of the precious grain.

Despite his earlier somber mood, Lynch encouraged the sailors' antics as they attempted to swim, float, and even sink in the water of the Dead Sea. He observed that a "muscular man floated nearly breast-high, without the least exertion."[227]

About sunset, they experimented with some of the horses and donkeys in the water. Could the animals swim as they did in the ocean, or would the weight of the water hold them down? The animals turned a little on their sides, they found, but didn't turn over, able to stay afloat. Their findings contradicted John Lloyd Stephens's account from earlier that year that horses panicked when put into the water. Perhaps Stephens's horses had been weak or exhausted.

Lynch had read extensively from classical scholars who had written about the sea:

Pliny says that some foolish, rich men of Rome had water from this sea conveyed to them to bathe in, under the impression that it possessed medicinal qualities. Galen remarked on this that they might have saved themselves the trouble, by dissolving, in fresh water, as much salt as it could hold in solution. . . . Galen was not aware that the water of the Dead Sea held other things besides salt in solution.[228]

That night a pleasant light wind came in from the west. "Blowing over the wilderness of Judea, it was unaccompanied with a nauseous smell."[229] Toward the next sunrise, though, the wind changed to the north and increased—as, of course, did the temperature. Sweeping along the western shore, the wind also acquired the fetid odor of the "sulphureous" marshes along that shore.

Sunday, April 30—Once again the Sabbath, Lynch allowed the men to sleep until the heat from the sun and the flies forced them awake. After the service, some of the men found quiet and refuge from the heat in deeper recesses of the ravine and observed the day in their own ways, some reading or writing and some sleeping.

Shortly after noon, they rowed across to the eastern side of the lake, with Lynch leaving the sharif with instructions to move the base camp to Ain Turabeh. Then, after dinner, they rowed a few miles up the eastern shore to their rendezvous below Kerak, the crusader citadel above the east side of the Dead Sea where Lynch had arranged to meet Sheikh 'Akil and his troops.

Kerak (or Al-Karak), built on a steep-walled bluff some three thousand feet above the sea, has commanded the region since biblical days, when it was a capital of ancient Moab. It was then called Qir-hareseth, or Kir-haraseth in the

King James version of the Bible, which describes an Israelite siege of the capital. King Mesha had failed to pay tribute, and the siege ended only after the king offered his son as a burnt offering. Assyrian ruler Ashurbanipal destroyed the Moab capital in the seventh century BC, but archaeological evidence indicates that it was repopulated, perhaps by Nabataeans from Petra. In the Byzantine era, a bishopric was located there, and it appears as a walled town on the Mataba mosaic map of sixth-century Christian landmarks, the oldest surviving map of the region.

For a time, the town disappeared from chronicles of the region, but crusaders built a fortified castle there in 1132, to protect a caravan route from Syria to Arabia and Egypt. In 1183, Saladin, founder of the Muslim Ayyubid dynasty, initiated attacks on the stronghold, then held by Rainald de Chantillon, and Saladin took control in 1188. The succeeding Mamluk dynasty enlarged the castle and built a tower, and the castle remained a crucial protection for the caravan route for centuries. In 1840, Egyptian Ibrahim Pasha destroyed much of the castle while capturing it, only to be starved out by the Ottomans four years later.

At the time of the Americans' visit, the castle remained a ruin, though remnants of the magnificent structure remained.

At five o'clock, when they had reached gunshot distance from the beach, Lynch spotted a Bedouin on the shore surrounded by cane and reeds, then several other men. Readying their guns in case of attack—though hoping for a welcome reception by waiting friends—the sailors put in for shore. They delighted to discover Jum'ah, one of 'Akil's men, whom the sheikh had sent to watch for them.

The Americans landed their boats on the beach and set up a camp near the stream emptying from Wadi Beni

JUM'AH, OF THE TRIBE EL HASSEE.

Sheikh 'Akil sent one of his men, Jum'ah, to watch for the American expedition boats on the beach below Kerak.

Hamed. From Jum'ah, they learned that after Sheikh 'Akil and his troops parted from the American expedition at Ain el Feshkah they had traveled to Salt, on the east side of the Jordan, to visit friends of the Beni Sakhr tribe. On the way, a group of Beni Adwans attacked. 'Akil had retreated before the larger force, losing his camels and baggage, but their Beni Sakhr friends joined them, and together they counter-attacked. 'Akil and his friends lost twelve men. The Adwans sustained twenty-one casualties, dead and wounded, including the death of the Adwan sheikh's son. Sheikh 'Akil had made it to Kerak, as agreed, though his surviving men and horses were much fatigued from the battle and subsequent journey.

That evening, Suleiman, the son of Abd' Allah, Christian sheikh of Kerak, and four other tribesmen arrived to invite the Americans to visit the mountain township, some seventeen miles away. 'Akil had dispatched them at daybreak, and they had observed the Americans' boats as they descended the winding paths through the foothills on the way to the sea.

The Muslim sheikh of Kerak had also sent an invitation, this one to visit the former crusader castle held by the Muslims. Kerak had both a Christian sheikh and a Muslim one, with an uneasy truce between them. A sizable Christian population, most of them Greek Orthodox, had immigrated from all over Palestine, with some from other parts of Syria, because of the relative tolerance shown them in Kerak.[230] The Christian sheikh Abd' Allah had some 250 armed men, but his Muslim counterpart had far more, which made the Christian leader subservient to the other. The Muslim townsmen, sometimes called Kerekin or Kerakîyehs, intermarried with the local Bedouin tribes, creating further strong ties.[231]

Because the sirocco had so seriously tapped his men's energy, Lynch chanced the edgy peace between the two sheikhs. He decided to transport the men to the mountain citadel for a rest and sent a request to 'Akil for horses and mules to convey the men through the foothills to the citadel.

The Christian Arabs from Kerak thrilled to see fellow Christians, shaking hands with great enthusiasm, and then, as was the custom, kissing their own hands used in the greeting. Except for Royal Navy commanders Charles Leonard Irby and James Mangles in 1818, Lynch and his sailors were the first undisguised Western Christians to visit Kerak since the Crusades. Ulrich Seetzen and Jean-Louis Burckhardt had visited earlier—but in disguise and speaking Arabic. The Christian Arabs exclaimed that, if they had known of the Americans' presence on the western shore, they would have traveled around the sea to visit them.

Lynch wondered if these "wild Arab Christians" of the tribe Beni Khallas or Beni Halasa ("Sons of the Invincible") descended from crusaders, the lost tribes of Israel, or remnants of early Christian groups who had escaped forced conversion by hiding in these inhospitable mountains. The Christians from Kerak knew that the Americans would sympathize regarding the persecutions that they endured under Muslim rule—and they were correct. Lynch wrote that the blood of his men boiled as they listened to the Christians' tales of woe.

After a refreshing bath in the nearby spring and dinner by firelight, Lynch set his sentries, and the sailors slept on the beach. Their new Arab friends also watched over them, a welcome precaution against the fear of nearby villagers and Bedouin wanderers. And they had reason for apprehension:

Jum'ah told Lynch that the sheikh of the nearby village had planned to attack the approaching boats, only changing his mind when Jum'ah told him that the sailors were Sheikh 'Akil's friends.

While they waited for 'Akil's transport to arrive, Lynch sent Dale and Aulick in the *Fanny Skinner* to finish their sketches of the bay and surrounding parts of the sea. Some of the men worked on the copper boat, which they discovered corroded rapidly in the salt water. Any scratch showed bright gold at first but then quickly tarnished when the air touched it.

One sailor asked a Kerak Christian if there were markets in their town to buy things.

"What we have we give," the man replied. "Do you think that we would sell you anything? You are our friends."

So the men turned their day of waiting into a feast day, and they dined sumptuously that afternoon on "wild boar's meat, onions, and the last of our rice."[232]

After the feast, Lynch borrowed a horse and rode out to look for ruins that Irby and Mangles had identified some thirty years earlier as Zoar, one of the Cities of the Plain destroyed by God's wrath. Lynch found "large heaps of stones in regular rows, as if they had once formed houses" and later a building foundation of some size, though rough cut.[233] The ruins appeared very old, but no columns or impressive features accompanied them. Though willing to assign Sodom to the muddy depths of the southern end of the Dead Sea based on the shallowness of the water, Lynch wasn't so quick to identify the jumble of rocks as Zoar.

Returning to the beach, he saw the mules and horses that he had requested. With them came Muhammad, the son of Abd'el Kadir, the Muslim sheikh, and Abd' Allah, the Christian sheikh. Muhammad was "about thirty years of age, very short but compactly built, with a glossy, very dark-mahogany skin, long, coarse black hair, and a thick, black beard and moustache. His eye, fiery, but furtive, was never fixed in its gaze, but, rolling restlessly from one object to another, seemed rather the glare of a wild beast than the expression of a human eye."[234]

Perhaps not surprisingly, he more favorably described Abd' Allah, the Christian sheikh, perhaps twenty years older: "a very different person; robust in frame, he was mild even to meekness." Lynch judged the differences in their demeanor as having come from "a long series of oppression on one side and submissive endurance on the other."[235]

Sheikh 'Akil sent a letter of welcome, making clear his friendship to all who heard it read aloud. The sailors entertained the dignitaries by launching one of their boats and sailing it back and forth with a few of the Arabs on board. Muhammad, the sheikh's son, declined to ride in the boat, which Lynch identified as a mark of cowardice. Those who did accompany the sailors stuck bits of onions in their nostrils to counteract the "bad air" from the sea, thinking the Americans madmen for spending so much time on "the sea accursed of God."[236]

That evening, from the distant darkness they heard the keening sound of Arab tribesmen, singing what could have been a song of welcome or a war-cry, long before the mounted Arabs wound into sight. Led by Muhammad's brother, the fourteen warriors carried long guns, with carbines slung low over their shoulders—except one. That man, also the sheikh's kinsman, balanced an eighteen-foot-long spear decorated with a bunch of ostrich feathers where the shaft joined the spearhead. The shrill sound continued as the horses pranced until the tribesmen finished the song. Only then did they dismount for ritual greetings.

That night, Lynch lay in the lee of a boat's awning, somewhat protected from the rising north wind, but again he couldn't sleep, turning over in his mind the expedition's perilous position. Muhammad and his eight companions had been joined by his brother and fourteen more men. Others, two or three at a time, continued to appear from the darkness until at least forty had gathered in the firelight. More might be hiding in nearby thickets. Earlier, Muhammad had strutted around as if he already held the sailors in his power. Should Lynch order his men to depart in the boats at first light and thus foil an unforeseen attack?

He hesitated. At his request, Sheikh 'Akil had traversed the whole of the dangerous eastern shore of the Dead Sea to bring provisions to the expedition—and 'Akil had vouched for the expeditioners, a people unknown in this region. If the Americans fled from danger now, what damage might that do to 'Akil, a friend who had lost men on his way to their rendezvous? What kind of reception from the Bedouin would the next Americans face if the sailors showed a lack of loyalty now? Moreover, Lynch's concern for his men hadn't lessened. Might some of them sicken and die without a break from the bad air and punishing heat of the Dead Sea? Without that rest, would the men's health prevent them from finishing their mission?

The sultry eighty-one-degree temperature turned into dew so heavy that it fell on the sailors' faces through the boats' awnings. This heavy dew had happened once before, so Lynch knew what was likely to follow—a sirocco—but not for hours. Hopefully, they would have reached Kerak by then.

Tuesday, May 2—After a hurried breakfast, they set off under cloudy skies, the sailors on donkeys and the officers on horses. Lynch left the boats with Jum'ah and Henry Loveland, the sailor least affected by the two weeks on the sea.

As they were leaving, the Christian sheikh revealed that Kerak Muslims, joined by another group of twenty, had planned to attack during the night. Lynch's vigilance through the night—frequently checking on his officer and the two sentries on guard, one positioned by the mounted blunderbuss—had convinced the aggressors that the Americans suspected their plan. The expedition party was small, and Lynch wasn't sure he could count on Mustafa, the cook, or others who weren't American. The sailors' weapons, however, were superior. Each had a breech-loaded carbine with a steel bayonet, as well as a pistol with an attached bowie knife. The officers had carbines but also swords equipped with pistol-barrels. They also importantly had twelve loyal mounted Bedouin and eight footmen as escorts. Without surprise on their side to even the odds, the tribesmen knew an attack would fail, and Bedouin famously didn't attack unless they thought they could win. Lynch's sleeplessness had saved their lives.

The Americans, Bedouin, and Kerak townsmen headed up the wadi, then wound around the base of the cliffs, and up the neck of a peninsula called Ghor el Mesraa el Kerak, which Seetzen had mistakenly identified as an island. They proceeded up Wadi Kerak, to the north of the peninsula, first through ruins of a city some suggested was the biblical Zoar but more likely was the crusaders' Zoghar.[237] The wadi tilted steeply upward, the trail sandwiched between a deep and dark chasm on one side, and on the other, rugged and undulating cliffs that resembled, even in their solemn colors, nothing so much as ocean storm waves transmuted into stone. Lynch avoided looking down into the abyss.

Within moments metaphor became reality. The caravan had started out under cloudy skies, but it soon began to sprinkle. Before they had gone halfway up the pass, thunder echoed from the cliffs, and showers began. A furious torrent of water swept "in a long line of foam down the steep declivity, bearing along huge fragments of rocks, which, striking against each other, sounded like mimic thunder."[238]

The rain rendered the trail even more perilous, but the storm passed as quickly as it had come. By mid-morning, the clouds and mist cleared enough for an amazing, though dizzying, view down the ravine.

When the group stopped for a break, the Kerak horsemen had some fun shooting at a mark. "Approaching to pistol shot distance and taking rest with their long guns, they rarely hit the mark. Their powder was so indifferent, that one of our sailors contemptuously remarked that a gazelle could run a mile between the flash and the report. They were perfectly astonished at the execution of our rifle."[239]

The trail crossed a wide terrace overlooking the valley, with the terrace interrupted here and there by huge sandstone rocks that had fallen so long ago from the rocks above that some of them had been hollowed to provide shelter from the elements. The soft stone was carved into houselike shapes, one even resembling a thatched cottage. The region bloomed beautifully with purple hollyhocks, oleanders, scarlet anemone, and other flowering plants. The caravan's movements startled partridges, doves, and other birds. A little later they passed cultivated wheat and some olive trees—but what would it have been like in those frightful days after the cataclysm that destroyed the Cities of the Plain? Certainly not like this.

When Lynch thought they must have reached the summit of the plateau, the trail forked, and he discovered that they had a long, steep hill to climb yet before reaching the walled city on the hill, the quadrangle tower to the northwest, part of the crusader fortress built in 1132. Even though much of what they could see had fallen into ruins—some of them perhaps dating back centuries—the skyline impressed them.

Though the Ottomans retained nominal control of Kerak, as in the rest of Palestine—Bedouin power was stronger than the Ottomans' on the east side of the Jordan. In recent years, various tribes had possessed the stronghold, with the Beni Sakhr and their allies the most frequent. In Kerak, Lynch's firman from the Ottoman Sultan carried less weight than the American's friendship with Sheik 'Akil, a Beni Sakhr ally.

Shortly after noon, the party crested the hill at the top of the plateau, reaching three thousand feet. Despite the fertility of the soil, the vista that they beheld consisted of grain and grass withered from locust blight and sirocco winds. They entered a gateway cut through the rock, through a passage that continued for 150 yards, and emerged into the walled town.

The houses consisted of unmortared stone, many of the mud roofs now occupied by residents craning their necks to see the Americans pass. Their escorts showed the men to the Christian schoolroom, which also served as the town's council chamber and a makeshift guesthouse. It was the same place where British officers Irby and Mangles had stayed in

The American sailors toured the ruins of the crusader castle at Kerak, constructed in the 1130s. *Watercolor by William A. Stewart, courtesy of the Victoria and Albert Museum, London.*

1818 during their tour of Palestine, the only other "Franks" to have visited the town, undisguised, since the Crusades.

The room contained nothing at all—just a bare stone floor and walls, with wooden rafters supporting the mud roof. No glass or shutters filled the two windows, and the rickety door wouldn't latch. Customarily, the townspeople would have killed a sheep for a feast to honor the visitors, but that didn't happen. The Christians, apparently, were too poor for such an extravagant entertainment. That the Muslim sheikh made no offer of hospitality, though, boded ominously. He clearly had an abundance of sheep.

Something was wrong.

With the Christian sheikh's help, the Americans bought eggs for their first meal in Kerak. The sailors took turns touring the sights. Lynch noted the castle, Krak des Moabites: "Partly cut out of, and partly built upon, the mountain-top . . . the remains of a magnificent structure. . . . Saracenic, although in various parts it has both the pointed Gothic and the rounded Roman arch."[240] The walls of the citadel, only partly standing in the 1840s, consisted of well-cut, heavy stones. The best-preserved part of the structure was the crusader chapel, especially the altar at the east end, with traces of fresco paintings amazingly still extant. Imagining this huge castle complex at the height of its power and glory in crusader times, with vast walls, five gates, and seven wells, amazed the expeditioners.

The condition of the chapel reinforced Henry Maundrell's conclusion in 1697 after touring over one hundred ruined churches in the Middle East:

> *Though their other parts were totally demolished, yet the east end we always found standing, and tolerably entire. Whether the Christians, when overrun by infidels, redeemed their altars from ruin with money; or whether even the barbarians, when they demolished the other parts of the churches, might voluntarily spare these, out of awe and veneration, or whether they have stood thus long, by virtue of some peculiar firmness in the nature of their fabric; or whether some occult providence has preserved them, as so many standing monuments of Christianity in these unbelieving regions, and presages of its future restoration, I will not determine.*[241]

Christians, when overrun by infidels, as Maundrell phrased it, survived by paying tribute to the Muslims, who mostly lived

190

in tents outside the walls. Like other towns that Lynch visited in Palestine, he described Kerak as filthy and squalid:

> *The males mostly wear sheepskin coats; the women, dark-colored gowns; the Christian females did not conceal their faces, which were tattooed like the South-Sea islanders. The priest, in his black turban and subdued countenance, acted as our* cicerone. *He took us to his little church, a low, dark, vaulted room, containing a picture of St. George fighting the Dragon; two half columns of red granite from the ruins of the castle, and a well of cool water in the center.*[242]

That evening, Lynch talked at length with 'Akil, who informed him that it was almost harvest time and southern Bedouin tribes were preparing for hostilities. As soon as the fellahin began harvesting grain, both the Beni Adwans and Beni Sakhrs would swoop in and carry it off, but each from villagers some distance away. Perhaps that was why the Muslim sheikh hadn't shown them the customary hospitality.

'Akil then hinted to Lynch some of his ambitions that would come to fruition in the coming decades. He was fishing for an expression of American imperialist interest in an alliance with the Bedouin tribes, presumably in rebellion against the Ottoman Empire. The Ottomans had already bought off 'Akil after his first successful rebellion, which was why he was present in the palace of the governor of Acre where Lynch met him.

Was 'Akil weighing possibilities for a wider insurrection? Lynch chose the words of his reply carefully, assuring 'Akil that, if he and his men had been captured, the sailors would have rushed to his aid; as the arrangement stood,

Lynch would endeavor to compensate 'Akil for the losses he had suffered in his battle with the Beni Adwans en route to assist the expedition.

However much Lynch might like the sheikh, he dared not let 'Akil embroil the expedition in the Bedouin conflicts with the Ottoman government or with each other, for he knew what censure he would face upon returning to America if he did. The sheikh could not think that, if he involved the expeditioners, their countrymen would come to his aid. What Lynch didn't know was that in the coming years 'Akil would become the major power in Galilee.

Changing the subject, wily 'Akil explained how, with so few men, he managed to assure the Kerakîyehs' good behavior. He had brought with him a prince of the Beni Sakhrs, a gallant warrior. Such diplomatic skills stood 'Akil in good stead now as it would again in the future.

'Akil also had a plan to avoid a repeat battle with the Beni Adwans on their return trip north. The sheikh and his men would take enough flour and water for a five- or six-day journey and head straight across the desert until they reached the pilgrim route to Mecca, then proceed north until they reached 'Akil's base near the Sea of Galilee.

'Akil might have assured Lynch of the Kerakîyehs' non-violence, but the next day Muhammad, the Muslim sheikh's son, continued his insolence and disrespect. The sheikh still hadn't invited the men to share a meal in his tents. The reason for this slight was slight itself. With his well-established abhorrence of bribery, Lynch disdained giving the sheikh a large present, the local custom, preferring to award gifts only for services or kindness—neither of which the Kerakîyehs had provided. Muhammad pressed Lynch for abas, a watch, or a gun, but Lynch—wisely or unwisely, depending upon how you view it—refused to allow Muhammad to intimidate him, even though the Kerak Muslims crowded their rooms, sometimes blocking the doorway, closely watching the Americans.

Irby and Mangles had been well treated in Kerak probably because they brought to the Muslim sheikh a letter of introduction from the sheikh of Hebron. But they also paid four hundred piastres—$1,600 in 1848. Burckhardt, who had come in the (probably not very good) disguise of a poor man, was extorted to the tune of 150 piastres, $600 then, and the tribe robbed Seetzen, also in disguise, even before he reached Kerak. Lynch was risking his life and that of his men with this stance of refusing to pay bribes, protection, or commissions, as others did. Indeed, he almost seemed to court a violent response.

When the Christians and the Kerakîyehs finally left the Americans to themselves that evening, the men propped up a board to support the unsecured door, enjoyed the luxury of a drink of sweet milk, and lay down under a roof for the first time in twenty-three days. Lynch lay awake, pondering what would happen the following day. 'Akil, their sponsor and ace card, had only four men with him, and one was wounded; the Kerakîyehs could marshal some seven hundred warriors.

The Christians couldn't afford to support the Americans because they would face dire consequences once the expedition departed. The Christians' situation had changed since so many of them had immigrated to Kerak, thinking it a safer place. They comprised three-quarters of the walled city's population and had some 250 fighting men among them, living in thrall to the Kerakîyehs, who dwelled in tents outside the town and preyed on their families, forcing them to provide a roof and food whenever the tent-dwellers came into town. The Kerakîyehs seized the Christians' property "without there being any one to whom to appeal; and remonstrance, on their part, only makes it worse."[243]

Many Christians had left Kerak because of these conditions, but those who remained were trying to build a new church in the hopes that it would bring the community together and sustain them. However, the sirocco and the locusts in recent years had decimated their once flourishing crops, and the Kerakîyehs took much of what was left.

The church leaders asked Lynch to carry a letter to sympathetic Christians in America, appealing for help. The letter was written in Arabic, but Lynch included a translation in his account of the expedition:

> *By God's favor!*
>
> *May it, God willing!, reach America and be presented to our Christian brothers,— whose happiness may the Almighty God preserve! Amen!*
>
> *We are, in Kerak, a few very poor Christians and are building a church.*
>
> *We beg your Excellency to help us in this undertaking, for we are very weak. The land has been unproductive and visited by the locusts for the last seven years. The church is delayed in not being accomplished for want of funds, for we are a few Christians surrounded by Muslims.*
>
> *This being all that is necessary to write to you, Christian brothers of America, we need say no more.*
>
> *The trustees in your bounty,*
> *Abd' Allah en Nahas, Sheikh,*
> *Yâkôb en Nahas, Sheikh's Brother.*
> *Kerak, Jâmad Awâh, 1264*[244]

The sailors rose early the next day, not having slept well due to the cold from the north wind that whistled through the casements, reminding them of home. Though they hadn't anticipated it, they had grown accustomed to the flea-free sand of the sea-beach. Still, the cool air, exercise of riding, and change of scenery had provided a healthy change, and the men behaved markedly less lethargic than before the Kerak excursion.

After a breakfast of eggs and rice, they prepared to leave. They would have liked to have stayed another day in the bracing Kerak air, but all the men sensed the Kerakîyehs' hostility increasing with each hour, making their presence there more and more unsafe. Muhammad tried to enter the guesthouse, but Lynch refused to speak to him. Shortly after, the sailors could see and hear the sheikh's son and several tribesmen in an animated discussion outside their windows.

Foolishly or confidently, Lynch firmly believed that 'Akil's affection, backed of course by the presence of his imported Beni Sakhr prince, would protect them—at least in Kerak. 'Akil had, with some difficulty, procured horses for the sailors. As the men were saddling up, Muhammad again approached with a demand for money, which again Lynch repulsed. The frustrated sheikh's son asked the sailors what they would do if they found one hundred men in their path. They could take care of themselves, Lynch replied.

At 6:30 a.m., carbines unslung and ready for immediate battle, the Americans left the makeshift guesthouse, accompanied by the Christian sheikh, who risked his life doing so. Lynch had scouted the path the day before and knew that the Kerakîyehs couldn't mount an effective attack unless part of their party lagged behind. Putting Lieutenant Dale in the lead of the caravan, Lynch took up the rear—the most dangerous position. Scarcely had they traveled a mile outside the town, when Muhammad, "black and surly," and a few of his followers on horseback caught up with them.[245] Lynch delighted at the turn of events. The game was now on his terms.

Lynch quietly detailed Midshipman Aulick and a seaman to shadow Muhammad and, regardless of his companions' actions, to shoot him if he showed any signs of treachery or flight. Muhammad did not immediately appreciate the shift in power, but slowly he showed awareness that whether he lagged behind, rode ahead, or even stopped, the same two Americans remained close by his side.

The tense atmosphere of the march dissipated somewhat when one of the donkeys, after a rest break, refused to allow his sailor to remount until the man borrowed a keffiyeh and tied it around his head like one of the Bedouin and also borrowed an aba.

When they spied the Dead Sea in the distance, shrouded by midday mist generated by heat-evaporated water, they had reached the twists and turns of the Wadi Kerak, the most dangerous part of the ride and the part most favorable to an attack. Not taking any chances, Lynch advanced to place himself at Muhammad's side. The young man's companions had left him, probably to join others riding out of sight as the caravan descended the ravine. The sheikh's son made no signal to his fellow tribesman, nor did he demand a watch, a gun, or money. When the caravan stopped for a rest about an hour from the beach, Muhammad even stooped to tighten Lynch's saddle girth—perhaps trying to curry favor or to save face by inducing the men to pay him tribute through kindness. Lynch interpreted the act as a sign of subservience.

They reached the beach and the waiting boats, and the men loaded their provisions. At the request of Abd' Allah, the

WADY MOJEB.

Wadi Mojeb, the biblical Arnon River, is distinguished by dramatic red sandstone water-carved into fantastic sculptural forms.

Christian sheikh, Lynch wrote a note to 'Akil, requesting his assistance in protecting the Christians, lest the Muslims vent their frustrations with the Americans upon them. To encourage the Beni Sakhr prince's support of the same cause, Lynch sent him an embroidered aba. He also gave the Christian sheikh a ceremonial gift in appreciation of his escort from Kerak. Muhammad he pointedly ignored.

But as Lynch was taking leave of Sheikh Abd' Allah, Muhammad made one last attempt at extortion, asking for gun-caps. Lynch refused because he knew that "the first use made of them would have been against a Christian."[246]

The sailors shoved off without regret.

XI

Leaving the Dead Sea

As the boats neared Wadi Mojeb, the biblical Arnon River, the steep, red sandstone cliffs bordering the sea grew beautifully variegated with yellow. A rock arch curved twenty feet above the water, spanning a twelve-foot channel. The stream widened again, and they stopped for the night at the mouth of the river, almost one hundred feet wide, bounded by cliffs carved by winter rains into fantastic sculptural forms.

In the sandy bottom of the ravine grew canes, tamarisk trees, and castor-beans, and the men observed camel tracks and remains of a Bedouin encampment. There must have been a hidden passage out of the ravine, even though the sides appeared too steep to climb. Lynch walked and waded up the passage for a considerable distance, identifying a dead gazelle and tracks of gazelles and other wild animals.

The sailors bathed in the fresh water, dined on tea and rice, and slept soundly on the boat awnings spread on the beach. At midnight, the thermometer measured seventy-eight degrees, which, after such prolonged exposure to heat, actually felt cold. One sailor in particular, George Overstock, was chilled, and Lynch feared that he might have come down with the fever notorious for affecting those who sailed on the Dead Sea.

The next morning, though, Overstock seemed better, and the boats set off on a warm morning after the men filled their water containers in the fresh-water stream. Overstock seemed better—but Lynch still worried.

Just as they were leaving, the sailors heard voices and two gunshots echoing through the canyon. They couldn't see any kind of disturbance or movement above, nor did they stop to search. Lynch sent the *Fanny Skinner* with Lieutenant Dale to sound across the sea to Ain Turabeh, while Lynch himself steered the *Fanny Mason* northward, near the western beach, with Aulick sketching the curves of the shoreline as they progressed.

While under way, Lynch conducted experiments with a thermometer, measuring water temperature at different depths. The water at 174 fathoms (1,044 feet) was 62 degrees, while at the surface it was 76 degrees. Curiously a stratum of cooler 59-degree water intervened at 10 fathoms. Otherwise, the change in temperature was gradual. Lynch hypothesized that crystallization might have been causing the increase in temperature at lower depths.

Later that morning they sighted the green vegetation of Ain Turabeh and the white tents at the base camp that they left in Sharif Hazzâ's charge. When they arrived, Hazzâ told

Lynch that he had heard of the battle between 'Akil's troops and the Beni Adwans. Several Beni Sakhr had since died of their injuries.

Lynch investigated the pass between the camp and the route to Jerusalem to determine whether it was suitable for surveying the levels between the Dead Sea and the Mediterranean. The route was steep but less so than other available routes, so they would begin their leveling there.

Lynch had purchased a new spirit level made by Troughton, a fine instrument of its day that surveyors used in a similar fashion to a theodolite to measure changes in elevation. Measurement involved men at two stations, the first at a position where they had already determined the altitude and the second some distance away—perhaps one hundred yards—but close enough to see a mark on a staff held by the second man. Analogous to a carpenter's level, the spirit level, using a moving bubble suspended in liquid, was attached to the eye-end of a telescope-like device. The spirit level was adjusted until the bubble centered over or between delicate wires, measuring the vertical change in altitude at the second location with great accuracy. The leveling—or measurement of changes in vertical altitude—was a slow and labor-intensive process, as the men proceeded up and down the landscape. As had been the case with so many men of science before them, one error could wreck the entire string of measurements. The recording proceeded slowly under Lieutenant Dale's watchful eye.

The men spent Sunday, May 7, resting, which they direly needed. The day before, with great effort, Lieutenant Dale, five seamen, and an Arab assistant leveled five hundred feet up the pass. Meanwhile, Midshipman Aulick returned after completing the mapping of the shoreline at the mouth of the Jordan—the only remaining task for creating a map of the sea. The mission was coming to an end.

That Sunday was blazing, the thermometer registering an incredible 106 degrees at 8:30 a.m. Sharif Hazzâ dozed in his tent, his Bedouin reclining nearby, while a heat-induced mist hung over the listless sea, nearly obscuring the opposite shore.

Surveyors calculating a change in elevation during the 1875–78 Palestine Exploration Fund mapping of Palestine. The American expedition used a similar process, but employed a Troughton spirit level to calculate angles, instead of a theodolite. *Drawing by Claude Reignier Condor, published in* Tent Work in Palestine: A Record of Discovery and Adventure, *1878.*

That evening a sirocco struck, felling the tents and breaking the second and only remaining siphon barometer. Fortunately, they had completed their measurement of the altitude of the Dead Sea with the instrument—though it would have been useful, for comparison, to confirm their calculation of altitude at the Mediterranean.

It took two hours for the hot blast of desert wind to decrease. When the temperature finally fell sufficiently, exhaustion helped the men to sleep. All day, the sailors had been lethargic. It was time to leave.

The Muslim call to prayer awoke Lynch the next morning, another sultry, cloudy day. The leveling party had surveyed over the pass the previous day and three hundred feet into the desert beyond. Today Lynch sent Lieutenant Dale to inspect the other side of the pass toward Jerusalem. He also sent two sick seamen to Mar Saba Monastery for treatment— Hugh Read and George Overstock, who hadn't entirely recovered from the illness that he had been fighting for the last several days.

Before departing the Dead Sea, Lynch took the *Fanny Skinner* out once more, this time to moor a flag platform that the sailors had constructed. He left the Stars and Stripes moored in eighty fathoms of water, too far from shore to be reachable by anyone without a boat. "The bonny flag floats gaily in the passing breeze, and, reflected upon by the sun, paints her colors upon that ocean, which covers the once beautiful plain, and magnificent cities of Sodom and of Gomorrah,"[247] one of the men wrote in his journal. Her mission complete, the iron *Skinner* was hauled ashore and disassembled, like her copper *Mason* companion, for camel transport to the Mediterranean and shipment home.

Some of the men bathed once more in the brackish water before retiring for their twenty-second and last night on the Dead Sea. Lynch no doubt lay awake that night, as he so often did on the mission, reflecting upon the expedition's accomplishments in their weeks at sea.

They had repeatedly sounded its depths. The soundings of the sea bottom showed that an underwater ravine continues the path of the Jordan River, with an average depth of about 1,300 feet. Moreover, at the south end of the sea, there is another deep ravine. Between these two deep ravines, though, lies a "sudden breakdown" or disruption in the path of the ravine leading from the Jordan to the deep ravine at the southern end. Because he wanted to believe, Lynch speculated that this disruption of the ravine represented "a plain sunk and '*overwhelmed*' by the wrath of God. . . . There can scarce be a doubt that the whole Ghor has sunk from some extraordinary convulsion; preceded, most probably, by an eruption of fire, and a general conflagration of the bitumen which abounded in the plain."[248] To his regret, he didn't have authorization to explore farther south, between the Dead Sea and the Red Sea, to test this theory. Though he knew that disbelievers would contradict his conclusions, he judged that the expedition had collected enough evidence to confirm "the truth of the Scriptural account of the destruction of the cities of the plain."[249]

The night passed quietly, with a light north wind that lulled even Lynch to sleep for a while by the sound of the waves lapping at the beach.

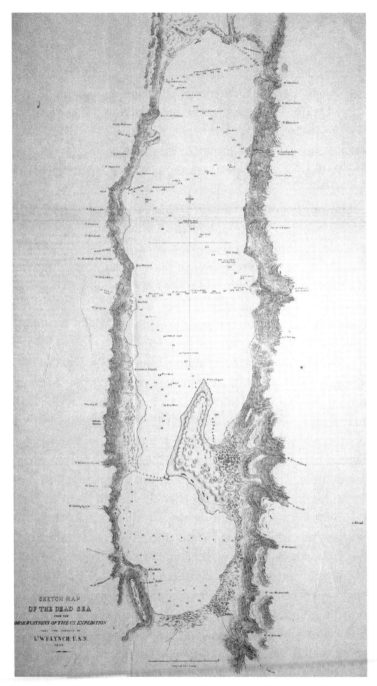

Lt. John Dale and Midshipman Richmond Aulick sounded the depths of the Dead Sea 162 times. Those measurements, crisscrossing the lake diagonally, proved invaluable in the future, appearing on other maps and serving as a record of water levels before the sea was diminished by the twentieth-century diversion of Jordan River water for irrigation and drinking water. *Courtesy of the University of North Texas Digital Library.*

Wednesday, May 10—The leveling party started that morning as usual under Lieutenant Dale's direction, while Lynch stayed behind to supervise the final striking of the camp. By 9:30, the men had struck the tents and loaded the equipment on six camels for the journey to Jerusalem.

With Lynch as he rode up the pass at Ain Turabeh came Sharif Hazzâ and the sheikhs from the Rashayideh and Ta'amirah Bedouin tribes, as well as a few of their men. As they wound up the mountainside, Lynch found himself, like Lot's wife, looking back at the site of their base camp and the silent sea. He wrote later of his sadness at parting with the now familiar people and places: "The feeling that we are never to see them again, makes us painfully sensible of our own mortality."[250] He knew it was unlikely that he would ever pass this way again. He never did.

The caravan caught up with the leveling party, and they stopped for the night just after 1:00 p.m. so as not to travel too far in advance of the slow-moving leveling group. They made camp in a ravine between the Bhuweir and en Nar wadis called Wadi Khiyam Seya'rah (Ravine of the Tents of Seya'rah), named for a Bedouin tribe surprised and slaughtered there. The expedition's Bedouin companions proved their worth once again when they dissuaded the men from camping in the cool, inviting caves on the north side of the ravine. According to the Arabs, the caves notoriously harbored scorpions and snakes that emerged at night.

That evening Lynch invited Sharif Hazzâ to the officers' tent. The older man was to part ways with them in the morning, so this was their last opportunity to learn from him what they could. Lynch cherished the sharif's friendship, which, he rightly believed, combined with 'Akil's, had prevented much bloodshed on numerous occasions.

Trading on the short length but tested strength of that friendship, Lynch asked the older man to tell his story as they sat around the campfire.

The sharif's father had been the hereditary governor of Mecca, and, upon the elder Hazzâ's death, the sharif's older brother had succeeded to the position. His brother's rule continued until Muhammad Ali conquered the state as part of his expansion across the Sinai and Arabia. Ali deposed the sharif's brother and placed a cousin on the throne in his stead, carrying Sharif Hazzâ back to Egypt where he languished in prison for a decade. When the Wahabis overran Arabia, Muhammad Ali released Sharif Hazzâ and gave him a military command, which ended when the European powers forced Ali to retreat back to Egypt in 1840.

That evening, a monk from the Mar Saba Monastery brought the news that the two sick sailors were recovering well. When everyone retired for the night, one of the Bedouin tribesmen loaned his aba to the monk, and so "the shaven-crown of the Christian and the scalp-lock of the Muslim were covered by the same garment."[251]

In the hilly wilderness of Judea, Lynch fell asleep thinking of how God had conversed with Abraham here and how John the Baptist preached salvation, preparing the way for Christ.

The night before, the cool of the high desert air caused the thermometer reading to plummet to sixty degrees, colder than the expedition had experienced in weeks. At first, the sailors delighted in the change in temperature, pulling their cloaks closer as the temperature dropped. But then, enfeebled as they had been by the heat of the last three weeks, the air began to feel piercingly cold, and they shivered intensely. The sentries were so busy finding firewood to feed the campfire, that "perhaps, in all our wanderings, the guard had never been so remiss."[252] Fortunately, danger lay far behind them, and no one chose this chilly moment for a sneak attack.

They breakfasted in the rocky ravine, gazing down upon the glassy surface of the Dead Sea from high above, then said their good-byes to the departing sharif. Still close enough to see the American flag waving in the breeze, the enlisted men may not have realized it, but Lynch's gesture of leaving a flag flying hardly represented a unique gesture. Citizens of the young United States of America proudly sported their flag all over the Middle East. John Lloyd Stephens, who originally had signed his travel narrative simply "An American Traveler" flew the Stars and Stripes as he sailed up the Nile. William H. Rau published a stereograph of a colleague, "E. Wilson Seated atop the Great Pyramid with American Flag Jacket." Miss Parks, an American traveler, during an overland journey from Jaffa to Jerusalem, attached a flag to her parasol, "taking possession as she called it of each place she passed through."[253] The sailors proudly left Old Glory flying, a claim—however tenuous—on the landscape. No one speculated about how long the raft would float before sinking or whether a fiercely gusting sirocco might topple the flag from its platform.

The next morning felt cool in comparison to the weeks at the Dead Sea, and the leveling party progressed up the Wadi en Nar (Ravine of Fire) near the Greek Orthodox monastery of Mar Saba. Barren limestone cliffs closed in the ravine, and the reflected sunlight and lack of any breeze made midday uncomfortably hot. Ever the romantic, Lynch found the setting bearable because the ravine formed an extension of the Kidron Valley; rain that fell on Jerusalem would, in the rainy season, rush in a torrent down the valley to this place on its way to join the heavy waters of the Dead Sea.

The venerable Greek Orthodox monastery of Mar Saba that overlooks the Kidron Valley has sheltered pilgrims since the fifth century AD. The convent's location is striking, with perpendicular cliffs on both sides and an approach through a terraced cliff face. Though the monks urged them to come inside, the sailors set up camp outside the monastery walls. They long ago had learned their lesson about fleas in Palestine's dwellings and declined.

> From the court we were led along a terraced walk, parallel with the ravine, with some pomegranate-trees and a small garden-patch on each side; and, ascending a few steps, turned shortly to the left, and were ushered into the parlor, immediately over the chasm. . . . The parlor was about sixteen by twenty-four feet, almost entirely carpeted, with a slightly-elevated divan on two sides. The stinted pomegranate-trees and the few peppers growing in the mimic garden were refreshing to the eye; and, after a lapse of twenty-two days, we enjoyed the luxury of sitting upon chairs.[254]

Within, they found their two sick-list men, whom the monks had treated, fully recovered and able to rejoin the expedition as it returned to the shores of its origin.

David Roberts's painting of the Greek Orthodox monastery of Mar Saba, overlooking the Kidron Valley. *Courtesy of the Library of Congress.*

On Monday, May 15, following a Sabbath day of rest, Lynch released from their duties of kindness all the Arabs, except for a guide and camel drivers. The caravan progressed along the western cliff overlooking the Kidron Valley, while the leveling party worked in the valley below, which involved fewer altitude changes.

About two hours into the journey, they came upon a large rock-hewn cistern, some twenty feet long, twelve feet wide, and eighteen feet high. The reservoir held about four feet of water, covered with green slime. Two Arabs were bathing in it. Admittedly, the water was hardly inviting, but in this water-scarce land, the Americans might not come upon more for some time. They watered their animals in it—and drank it themselves.

The moment afforded Lynch time to reflect on the contrast between his surroundings in the Ottoman Empire and his home state of Virginia in the same season. "There, hills and plains, as graceful in their sweep as the arrested billows of a mighty ocean, are before and around the delighted traveler." But here in parched Palestine, the prevalent color was dull-brown, "the color of ashes." For Lynch, the contrast was clear, "The patriot may glory in the one, the Christian of every clime must weep, but even in weeping, hope for the other."[255]

As the leveling advanced, they reached a valley that to their eyes, unaccustomed for so long to any great expanse of green vegetation, appeared beautiful. A village perched on a hill overlooking fields, and townspeople gathered, pointing toward the caravan. Some people came down to talk to the Americans, saying that they would not permit the camel drivers to pass because those men came from another tribe. They demanded that the expedition use camels and camel drivers belonging to the village—and, of course, pay for them. Ever opposed to bribery and extortion, Lynch ignored them, crossing to the other side of the valley to set up camp.

The next day, Lieutenant Dale's party began its leveling duties again at daybreak. Soon, the sheikh of the village, with fifteen or twenty men armed with long guns, approached Lynch and demanded money for the privilege of passing through the village's land. Lynch refused, as he had the day before, and the two parties exchanged loud words in their two languages. The inventive sheikh tried a different tactic, presenting the Americans with a sheep, for which he then refused payment. Lynch quickly perceived the rules of the game and knew the sheikh wanted an exorbitant price for the sheep. Determined not to humor him, Lynch paid a fair price for the animal, and the sheikh left disappointed.

When the confrontation had abated, the sailors enjoyed the pastoral scene. In every direction, shepherds' raised voices in Arabic mingled with the noises of goats, sheep, and cattle. In the fields, reapers were harvesting, and at a thresh-ing floor, three oxen, harnessed side by side, trampled the grain as the donkeys of the Ta'amirah Bedouin had done in Ein Gedi. The methods were primitive, but here the people had cultivated every inch of the fertile valley. Only the pres-ence of armed fellahin guarding the fields from attack broke the atmosphere of bucolic serenity.

The caravan came to a narrow ridge, and on the other side lay thirty or forty black Bedouin tents. A nearby red stain on a rock, according to their guide, indicated a blood tale. A Bedouin widower had eloped with a married woman from the encamped tribe before them—an exceptional crime. In less than a month, though, the woman had died. Knowing that he could be put to death for adultery should he happen upon a member of the woman's family, the offender pur-sued a settlement. The price to end the feud was steep—his daughter, a camel, some sheep, and four hundred piastres to the cuckolded widower—but the adulterer agreed. A feast cemented the deal, but the woman's first husband continued to brood. One day he saw the second man approach, and he shot him. According to Bedouin custom, because of the breach of faith, both tribes had an obligation to find and kill the murderer.

It's a strange and personal anecdote to have included in his narrative of the expedition. Why did this story of Bedouin lust and betrayal, retold at length, fascinate Lynch so much? Throughout Palestine, he had observed the nomadic culture of the Bedouin and identified with their code of honor. But there was something more to his telling—what awaited Lynch when he returned home.

He was in the midst of divorce proceedings. In the divorce trial, which would last five years—including the time he spent in Palestine—he accused his wife of "wantonness," substantiated by witnesses who described her extramarital affairs to the court while Lynch was away at sea. It was rumored that she had had an affair with one of his brothers, and it is entirely possible that Lynch proposed the Palestine expedition partially to escape the unpleasant situation, to which, as he listened to the Bedouin blood tale, he knew he was about to return.

XII

Jerusalem Again

In 1848, travelers had to have strong motivation to undertake the arduous and often dangerous journey to Jerusalem, the holy city on the hill. Religion usually provided the impetus, passionate faith tempting foreigners to endanger their mortal lives in the interest of saving their souls.

Gaza and Acre possessed the only ports in Palestine, but most pilgrims traveling from the coast chose to disembark at Jaffa, though doing so meant jumping into the waves and wading ashore. If the pilgrims were well–to-do or afraid of drowning, they hired a rowboat. The biblical importance of Jaffa, inhabited long into prehistory, lay in its association with the embarkation point for the prophet Jonah's encounter with the whale. Pilgrims chose the uncomfortable

Jaffa-to-Jerusalem route, though, not because of Jonah but because it offered the shortest distance from the coast, and every additional mile overland increased the risk of being robbed or killed.

A narrow coastal plain rising through barren foothills to a mountainous spine, Palestine's geography easily revealed travelers to all-watching eyes. Abu-Ghosh, a village that controlled one of the main routes to Jerusalem, for example, was often called the "robber's village"—after what was thought to be the main occupation of its townspeople. Pilgrims routinely purchased "protection" that, in theory, gave them safe passage. Because of shifting loyalties between villages and Bedouin tribes allied with the rival Qaysi[256] and Yamani factions, though, protection was best procured for short distances.[257]

Lynch and his men approached from the east, not the west, though. If anything, the landscape that they traversed proved even more dangerous than the route of ordinary pilgrims from the coast, especially because Lynch refused to pay for protection. If the sailors hadn't been so heavily armed, they, like earlier European travelers, such as Burckhardt and Seetzen, might have fallen prey to attacks.

After they circled a Bedouin encampment, Lynch left the caravan for a moment and rode to the top of a hill where he glimpsed, at the head of the Kidron and Hinnom Valleys, the walls and rooftops of Jerusalem hovering above. As he paused there, gazing upon the holy city, he felt an awareness as never before of the hallowed nature of the geography of redemption.

What a contrast. Behind Lynch lay the Dead Sea, the site of God's ultimate destruction, a watery mantle that He had thrown over cities that He had destroyed. Many believed that no one could sail on the Dead Sea and live, but Lynch and his men had proved the legend wrong—so far.

Though still so close that rain falling at this location would flow four thousand feet downhill and twenty miles into the deadly body of water behind, Lynch could see Jerusalem, the City of the Great King, shining above. Here at hand lay the Valley of Jehoshaphat, the appointed place where God would gather all nations on Judgment Day.

History's millennia had softened and mellowed the ultimate city on the hill, sunlight glancing off its limestone buildings. Like all the ancient cities of Palestine, Jerusalem was walled, a protection not only against siege by conquering armies but also from the day-to-day bands of marauders that preyed upon both travelers and townspeople. In 1848, Jerusalem had yet to grow beyond its walls. Above the ancient ramparts, near the middle of the city, stood the glittering gold of the Dome of the Rock, the seventh-century mosque built by the Umayyad caliph Abd al-Malik on the ruins of the second Jewish temple, destroyed by the Romans in AD 70.

Self-consciously, Lynch felt his "feeble pen" unworthy of describing all he saw and felt, especially after so many others had depicted the same experience of approaching the city and its holy wonders. Everywhere he went in this foreign yet familiar land, the reality of the present assaulted his senses, competing for notice with a second, shadowy world, the world of the Scriptures that took place thousands of years earlier in the same landscape. A believer, Lynch saw this shadow world of biblical events as no dry history lesson; he held it closely, in emotion-tinged detail, built up in his mind over decades and as visual as his own adventures. He had

Jerusalem in the distance, painted by David Roberts. *Courtesy of the Library of Congress.*

been preparing for this moment since early childhood. It was as if he had been to Jerusalem before.

Edward Robinson articulated this same feeling of kinship with the city: "From the earliest childhood, I had read of and studied the localities of this sacred spot; now I beheld them with my own eyes; and they all seemed familiar to me, as if the realization of a former dream. I seemed to be again among cherished scenes of childhood, long unvisited, indeed, but distinctly recollected."[258]

After his glimpse of the holy city, Lynch described a more prosaic landscape as the expedition drew nearer to Jerusalem. They passed through carefully cultivated "fields of yellow grain, orchards of olives and figs, and some apricot-trees."

The barren hillsides grew nothing at all, no trees, not even bushes. However, most of the slopes bore vestiges of terraces, indicating that the land had sustained crops of one kind or another in ages past. Continuing up the valley, the vegetation grew increasingly verdant: the "dark hue of the olive, with its dull, white blossoms, relieved by the light, rich green of the apricot and the fig, and an occasional pomegranate, thickly studded with its scarlet flowers."[259] The caravan stopped for a drink of cool, delicious water at Job's Well. A small, arched stone hut protected the well shaft, which they measured—118 feet deep.

Everywhere he looked, Lynch visualized Old Testament stories. There the aging Solomon, to please his foreign wives, denied the true God by worshiping Ashtaroth, goddess of the Sidonians, and Molech, god of the Ammonites. Farther up the Kidron Valley, he identified the site of the gardens of the kings of Israel. Nearby he noticed Absalom's cut-rock tomb with its conical roof. They turned left, continuing uphill through the Valley of the Son of Hinnom, where, according to legend, Saul was anointed king. They passed the Aceldama, the potters' field that Judas bought with pieces of silver and the site of the pool where King David saw Bathsheba bathing.

The present intruded upon Lynch's identification of Old Testament sites as his officers surveyed changes in elevation as they skirted Mount Zion. He didn't forget, though, that it was up Mount Zion "that Abraham, steadfast in faith, led the wondering Isaac," to offer his son as a blood sacrifice.[260]

Oddly, though Lynch describes the landscape in exhaustive detail and occasionally mentions the expedition's official purpose—to survey the altitude as they proceeded up and down between the Dead Sea and the Mediterranean—he

TOMB OF ABSALOM.

The cut-rock tomb of Absalom with its distinctive conical roof was one of the Jerusalem sites that inspired Lynch and other sailors to visualize events of the Old Testament.

makes little reference at all to Jerusalem's inhabitants. It's almost as if he has turned a blind eye to the present, so intent is he on the biblical past. He sees the landscape—but only to imagine locations as they were thousands of years before.

According to an 1838 census, the Jerusalem of the time had a population of some fourteen thousand inhabitants, with approximately three thousand Jews.[261] By comparison, Paris at mid-century had over 1 million residents and New York more than half a million. As one historian commented of Palestine at the time, "Nowhere else in the world were there cities so gigantic in their symbolic meaning for so much of humanity, yet so insignificant in purely physical terms."[262]

Holy to all three Abrahamic faiths—Judaism, Christianity, and Islam—Jerusalem, territorially belonging to the Ottomans, fell under Muslim law, which regarded Jews and Christians as "peoples of the Book." God had revealed himself to them, but, Muslims believed, Christians and Jews had rejected the ultimate revelation of the prophet Muhammad. Still, if they paid a special tax, they bought themselves a degree of protection—despite living under severe restrictions. Christians had a greater degree of protection because of the power of their sects in other countries, but until the 1830s, when foreign powers first began to take an interest in the return of Jews to Palestine, Jews had no political recourse.

Regulations dictated that at shrines sacred to all three religions, Muslims had precedence. For example, a mosque had been constructed over the cave believed to contain the remains of patriarchs Abraham, Isaac, and Jacob, as well as matriarchs Sarah, Rebecca, and Leah; Jews were barred from entering the mosque and could climb only the first seven steps outside. Nor were Jews allowed on the Temple Mount, site of the destroyed second temple, where the Dome of the Rock now stood. They could pray at the Western Wall, the remnant of the ancient wall surrounding the temple—sometimes called the Wailing Wall from the fervor of their prayers—but Muslims could, without penalty, throw garbage on their heads from the Temple Mount above.[263]

Many Americans chafed quietly at a Jerusalem ruled not only by non-Protestants but by non-Christians. William M. Thomson, for example, a missionary in Palestine for some forty years, tried to popularize the idea that Protestants had a special claim upon Palestine that supplanted non-Christian claims. Just as Abraham, leader of the Israelites, God's first chosen people, had a God-given right to claim Canaan, so did Protestants, legitimate heirs to Abraham by faith, he believed, have a God-given right to establish a presence in the Holy Land unhindered by Muslims or Jews.[264] Edward Robinson's tremendously popular books also promoted quasi-political claims to Palestine that made sense to Americans who viewed the dying Ottoman Empire as an inefficient caretaker with no real claim to the region.[265]

Palestine was central to the widespread nineteenth-century American belief in millennialism, the idea that a thousand-year golden age would precede the return of Christ. Early millennialism advocated both the return of Jews to Palestine and their conversion as essential for the golden age, but by Lynch's time religious leaders, such as Daniel Whitby, Jonathan Edwards, Elias Boudinot, and others, had promulgated the idea that Christianity would spread through the world gradually, over time. William Blackstone argued for the restoration of the Jews even before their conversion, as well as for the redemption of the Palestinian landscape—into Protestant hands, of course—prior to the golden age. Samuel Hopkins preached that the beginning of the millennium could be achieved if leaders were willing to act from "disinterested benevolence," meaning the willingness to take risks for the improvement of all people, not just believers.[266] Lynch's mission to the Dead Sea, though technically secular, fell into line with this late-millennialist theology. He was willing to risk life and limb in a seemingly quixotic adventure, to prove the veracity of the Bible, which he believed would inspire repentance and conversion.

Lynch's narrative about the expedition bristles with the expansionism of the post–Mexican-American War era. He had asserted that "fifty well-armed, resolute Franks, with a large sum of money, could revolutionize the whole country."[267] He had neither fifty soldiers nor a large sum of money, but readers of his tale could participate vicariously in his symbolic appropriation of the Holy Land. Lynch's patriotic fantasies by no means stood alone. Bayard Taylor said of the Plain of Sharon, "Give Palestine into Christian hands, and it will again flow with milk and honey."[268] The expedition unwittingly assisted the British in their own mapping of Palestine, which took on increased importance for British colonial ambitions. In the end, it was the "resolute Franks" of European powers, not Americans, who revolutionized the country. But while Lynch and his sailors trod the cobblestones of Jerusalem, it was by no means clear where American ambitions regarding Palestine might lead.

The expedition camped for several days about a mile and a half from the city, outside the Jaffa Gate, so that the officers and men could take turns touring the city assisted by a paid guide. They traversed the narrow, labyrinthine streets of the ancient city, essentially still the pattern laid out by Romans in the second century AD. Now, stone houses and shops, sometimes several stories high, cut off daylight and created an atmosphere that Lynch described as "gloomy grandeur."[269]

The youngest member of the expedition, perhaps Lynch's son, Francis, gave his reactions of his first venture into the city:

The Via Dolorosa, or Sorrowful Way, first arrested our attention, and our guide pointed out the spot where our Savior fell under the burthen of his cross. A little farther on, we had a partial view of the mosque of Omar, above the high walls by which it is surrounded. While we gazed upon it, a crowd of Abyssinian pilgrims called out to us with such fierce expressions of fanatic rage that our hands instinctively grasped our weapons. The movement had its effect, and after indulging our curiosity, we passed on unmolested.[270]

They walked through a gate, descended a length of stairs, and came to the court in front of the Church of the Holy Sepulcher, which they found crowded with "motley groups of Jew peddlers, Turks, beggars, and Christian pilgrims." Lynch took pity on a cripple and gave him a piaster, which immediately resulted in cries of "baksheesh! baksheesh!" from a host of beggars who surrounded Lynch and his companions. Their guide had to use his stick to force a path to escape the throng.

The Church of the Holy Sepulcher disconcerted most travelers. Instead of the cathedral that they anticipated, they found a jumbled assortment of chapels dedicated to competing Christian sects, all crowded in one building. "All is glitter & nothing is gold," Herman Melville wrote about his visit to the portion of the church reputed to be Christ's tomb.

"A sickening cheat."[271] Lynch's impression reads more tact-fully: "The lights, the noise, and the moving crowd had an effect for which the mind was not prepared, and with far less awe than the sanctity of the place is calculated to inspire, we entered the sepulcher."[272]

Curiously, Lynch accepts uncritically the identification of holy sites such as the Holy Sepulcher by Catholic and other Christian sects with long histories in Palestine, something other prominent Protestants visiting the area in the mid-nineteenth century did not do. Indeed, widely read Protestant writers such as Edward Robinson and William M. Thomson obsessively discussed and disparaged the earlier—usually Catholic—characterizations of holy sites and also, surpris-ingly, the interpretations of their fellow Protestant writers.

Robinson, though, wanted to do more than debunk or criticize; he developed a method of identifying holy sites for Protestants that involved close reading of the Scriptures, his-torians such as Josephus, and early Christian writers like St. Jerome and Eusebius, as well as archaeological research and an examination of Arabic place names for linguistic and geo-graphic connections. Robinson explained:

> Time and time again we visited the more important spots and repeated our observations; comparing meanwhile what we had seen ourselves with the accounts of ancient writers and former travelers, until at length conjectures or opinions were ripened into conviction, or gradually abandoned. Our motto was in the words, though not exactly the sense, of the Apostle: "'Prove all things, hold fast that which is good.'" During the same interval, I also took many measurements both within and around the city.[273]

The crowded interior of the Church of the Holy Sepulcher, rather sanitized in David Roberts's 1836 depiction. *Courtesy of the Library of Congress.*

Not unlike Lynch, Robinson portrays himself as a combination of skeptical modern empiricist and a worshipful, timeless pilgrim, measuring tape in hand, asserting that he arrived at his results in the interests of religious knowledge.[274]

Lynch had read Robinson's book and was familiar with his methods but personally saw no need to agonize over the precise present locations of holy sites. Rather, the shadowy presence of the biblical past, as he imagined it, seemed more important:

> *Most of the wall, and all the houses of Jerusalem, were demolished by Titus. Who, therefore, can believe in the assigned localities along the "Via Dolorosa"? Who can credit that here the Virgin Mary was born; there, the Savior instituted the sacrament of the last supper; or that yonder is the house where Pilate sat in judgment? Faith does not require, and true reverence would not be sustained by, such weak credulity.*[275]

Even about the controversial Church of the Holy Sepulcher, he said: "If it does not cover all the sacred localities assigned to it, some, at least, may lie beneath its roof, and none can be very far distant from it"—a very practical response from someone so intent on proving the geography of the Hebrew scriptures.[276]

Lynch chose not to discuss the current dismal conditions in Jerusalem or Palestine's future prospects, though he gave his opinion that both the number and fanaticism of the Ottomans were diminishing, as both Jewish and Christian populations were increasing—at least in Jerusalem. Bedouin unrest troubled him, but he foretold a sea change there, too, that would come like a "political sirocco."[277] He knew enough of international politics to know that the major nations in Western Europe—Britain, France, Prussia, and Austria—were pondering the "Eastern Question" (what to do if the Ottoman Empire collapsed), especially as it related to Russian ambitions and their own balance of power.

Upon the destruction of the Ottoman Empire, which must come in the not too distant future, a barrier would fall, he foresaw, that prevented the restoration of the Jews to Palestine. After that, Lynch hoped, would come what sounded like a golden age: "The increase of toleration; the assimilation of creeds; the unanimity with which all works of charity are undertaken, prove, to the observing mind, that, ere long, with every other vestige of bigotry, the prejudices against this unhappy race will be obliterated by a noble and a God-like sympathy."[278]

Monday, May 22—Lynch had settled the expedition's accounts with the American consul, Mr. Finn. The sailors broke camp, loading the remaining equipment on mules, rather than camels, and Lynch ordered his officers to proceed with running the line of the level the thirty-three miles to the Mediterranean.

At 1 p.m., they began from the benchmark that they had carved into a cliff face northwest of the city. The road from Jerusalem to the coast, like so many others in Palestine—really more of a camel or donkey track—was "execrable," so the exacting, laborious work of skirting hills and cresting passes continued unabated.

The sailors hoped for one last view of Jerusalem, but intervening hills concealed the holy city. They camped for

the night at Ain Dilbeh (Fountain of the Plane-Tree), a spring nestled in an oak grove. Their guide pointed out a ruin on a hill, which he identified as the castle of the Maccabees. Somewhere nearby, Lynch speculated, the Virgin Mary would have visited Elizabeth, John the Baptist's mother.

They followed the Frank road to the left, used by Napoleon on his march to Gaza. Several farmers worked nearby fields, and in the morning a group of wandering dervishes with banners and a few Christian pilgrims passed them on the way to the coast. Turning west, the caravan traversed some sand hills and, finally, planted the level on the beach of the Mediterranean, about one and a half miles from Jaffa.

Using the triangulation method, Lynch determined the level of the Dead Sea to be 1316.7 ft. below sea level (1235.589 Parisian ft. or 401.24 meters).[279] Though it is impossible to know what the exact level was at any date in the nineteenth century, due to fluctuations caused by rainfall or season, Cippora Klein's reconstruction of the sea's level in the nineteenth century puts the sea at 399.5 meters below sea level—extremely close to Lynch's measurement.[280] Lynch himself did not view his determination of the Dead Sea level to be definitive, rather stating that the expedition's "result is confirmatory of the skill and extraordinary accuracy of the triangulation of Lieutenant Symonds, R.N."[281]

However, it was not only the near-accuracy of Lynch's numerical figure that mattered; it was also the lack of errors or any confusion about his methodologies. Unlike all previous expeditions, the Lynch expedition, using the dual methodologies—both barometric calculation of atmospheric pressure and also triangulated measurement of the level—encompassed no errors or confusion. He did not, for example, make de Bertou's error of calculating that the level of the

Red Sea was 630 feet different from the ocean, an impossibility because the Red Sea connects to the ocean. Nor did he make Lieutenant Symonds's mistake of miscalculating the level of the Sea of Galilee, which threw his Dead Sea calculations into question. No. The Royal Geographical Society did not give Lynch a gold medal, nor declare him the winner of the race to determine the altitude of the Dead Sea. Rather, the American contribution was to verify the accuracy of previous measurements that were not considered definitive. That, for the Americans, seemed to be enough.

Lynch proudly described the expedition's accomplishment:

> *We had carried a line of levels, with the spirit-level, from the chasm of the Dead Sea, through the Desert of Judea, over precipices and mountain-ridges, and down and across yawning ravines, and for much of the time beneath a scorching sun. It had been considered by many as impracticable. It has, however, been accomplished; and with as much accuracy as, I believe, it can be done.*[282]

The primary tasks of the expedition completed, the sailors headed for a rest at the seaside country house of the consular representative before their return journey to Beirut and home.

Epilogue

After the expedition's official mission had ended, its members rested a few days. The land party, under Lieutenant Dale, headed north along the coast for a three-day ride to Acre that passed through the ruins of Herod's port at Caesarea, while Lynch and the remaining sailors took a chartered brig.

When the land party was about halfway to Acre, seaman Charles Horner incurred the only major injury of the expedition when he accidentally shot himself in the arm. Dr. Anderson had already parted from the expedition, so volunteer Henry Bedlow somehow managed to save Horner's life by fashioning a pressure bandage to stanch the flow of blood. Dale sent the two ahead to Acre in a chartered felucca, a small two-masted sailing vessel.

When the groups reunited in Acre, Lynch immediately sent Horner with Midshipman Aulick, Bedlow, and three other sailors to Beirut to seek treatment for Horner's injury. The others, under Lynch's command, set off on a meandering route toward Beirut that included Nazareth, Mount Tabor, and the Sea of Galilee. Before their earlier journey down the Jordan River, Lynch had commissioned the building of a wooden boat so that they could explore the Sea of Galilee upon their return. They discovered, to their distress, that the boat would not be finished for another two weeks. Unable to wait, the expedition continued instead around

SOURCE OF THE JORDAN.

Lieutenant Lynch planned the expedition's return route from Jerusalem to Beirut so that they passed by the source of the Jordan River. Lieutenant Dale thought that the scene made "a more beautiful picture than any he had ever beheld."[283] He sketched it with Prince Ali in the foreground.

the western shore of the lake to Capernaum and then to the entry of the Jordan River into the lake. Guided by Prince Ali Shehab, whom Lynch describes as a member of one of the oldest families in Syria, they reached the source of the Jordan. Lynch described the scene:

> We came suddenly to the source, a bold, perpendicular rock, from beneath which the river gushed copious, translucent, and cool. . . . The hand of art could not have improved the scene. The gigantic, all majesty, above; its banks, enameled with beauty and fragrance, all loveliness, beneath; render it a fitting fountain-head of a stream which was destined to lave the immaculate body of the Redeemer of the world.[284]

231

While on the snowy summit of Mount Hermon, Lynch tried to use their one remaining apparatus for ascertaining altitude, because their three mountain barometers had broken, but he discovered the scale attached to the boiling water apparatus failed because it was not properly graduated. He had to settle for a reading of "about 9,000 feet," which he thought might be "a little more than the actual height."[285] This estimate fortunately didn't affect the credibility of his determination of the level of the Dead Sea by barometer and triangulated leveling.

Joined again by Bedlow and Aulick, they headed toward an arduous route through the mountains to Damascus, Baalbek, and Beirut on the coast. As they left Damascus, the long road ahead, some of the men complained of not feeling well. Lynch hoped the cooler mountain air might improve their health, but it did not. He shortened the journey as much as he could, leaving out an extensive exploration of the Roman structures at Baalbek and a tour of the massive cedars of Lebanon.

Lynch began to think that his sailors had "imbibed the disease which has heretofore prostrated all who have ventured upon the Dead Sea." Looking at his "companions drooping" around him, he reproached himself for proposing the Dead Sea expedition.[286] Perhaps proving the curse right after all, Lieutenant Dale succumbed to their unidentified ailment, which might have been influenza contracted in Damascus, from the global pandemic of 1847–48, complicated by pneumonia.[287] He died at Eli Smith's mountainside villa near Beirut, the only death among the American sailors during the expedition. The others recovered and returned to America.

They arrived back at Hampton Roads, Virginia, on the USS *Supply* on December 8, 1848, and the crew was paid, with the exception of Horner, who went to a receiving ship for treatment of his injured arm. Lynch began work on a narrative about the voyage, with two months of assistance from Midshipman Aulick, who continued his naval career and was later named lieutenant commander in 1865.[288]

Henry Anderson did not return to America with the other members of the expedition, though later he made New York his home and became a trustee of Columbia College. He continued to travel and participated in another naval expedition, this one in 1874 to the South Seas, to observe a rare astronomical event. Afterward, he traveled to India, contracted cholera in the Himalayas, and died in Hindustan in 1875.[289]

RUINS OF BAALBEC.

Lynch cut short his planned examination of the Roman ruins at Baalbek because several of his sailors had fallen ill.

Sheikh 'Akil, in the years following his adventures with the American expedition, became an increasingly powerful chieftain. Though he spent a year in an Ottoman prison, in the 1850s he became the de facto ruler of Galilee, protector of Christians and Jews, and an intimate of several European consuls. It was not until 1864 that the Ottomans fielded enough Kurdish machineries to unseat him and regain control of Galilee.[290]

In early 1849, while Lynch was still working on his narrative, a rival book about the voyage, *Narrative of the Late Expedition to the Dead Sea. From a Diary by One of the Party*, was published. *Supply* hospital steward Edward P. Montague, who stayed on the ship rather than participating in the expedition, had edited it. Apparently, he based his book on one or more diaries of the seamen, perhaps supplemented by interviews. Lynch need not have worried much about Montague's book, which received uniformly negative reviews as being superficial. It only increased public anticipation of Lynch's own book on the expedition.

Lea and Blanchard in 1849 published Lynch's *Narrative of the United States' Expedition to the River Jordan and the Dead Sea* with a gold-stamped embossed cover, twenty-eight wood engravings based on deceased Lieutenant Dale's original drawings, and two foldout maps, one of the Dead Sea and the other of the whole of Palestine. The book won critical praise. The *New York Commercial Advertiser* called Lynch's style "altogether agreeable" with "an imaginative glow and a high poetic tinge." The *Boston Post*, though, said he invested "the most common occurrences with adjectives and pomposity."[291] The public judged the book favorably, and it appeared in nine American, six British, and two German editions.

A few years later Charles Scribner published Lynch's memoir of his early naval career, *Naval Life, or Observations Afloat and on Shore: The Midshipman;* and in 1852 the US Navy issued *The Official Report of the US Expedition to Explore the Dead Sea and River Jordan.*

Lynch's naval career flourished as well, and, after courts finalized his contentious divorce, he married Elisa D. Lochhead, another Virginian, though the marriage certificate does not survive.[292] In 1849, he became a commander, and in 1850, a captain. In 1849, while working on the official report, he proposed commanding a rescue mission for John Franklin's disappeared arctic expedition, but was unable to convince the navy to support the endeavor.[293] In 1852, he did receive permission to head another expedition, this time to explore trade and commercial potential in north-central Africa, which resulted in another publication issued by the navy in 1853, *Report in Relation to the Coast of Africa.*

Like many other Virginians in 1861, when the Civil War appeared imminent, he resigned his commission, first to serve as a captain in the Virginia Navy, then the Confederate Navy. He held several commands, including the defense of Roanoke Island as well as leading Southern forces during the Union attack on Fort Fisher in North Carolina. After the war, he was paroled in 1865, dying later that year in Baltimore, Maryland.

Lynch and his sailors, in their Palestine adventures, acted out the fantasies of thousands of American Protestants. They sailed upon the Sea of Galilee, visited Jesus's baptismal site on the Jordan, and investigated the mysterious Dead Sea. The primary source of these fantasies, which included castles and temples, lush palm-tree oases, and sand dune deserts, of course, was the Bible.

The Jordan River and the Dead Sea frequently appeared in scriptural narratives: the crossing of the Israelites into the Promised Land and the baptism of Jesus by John the Baptist, among many others. Along with God's wrath and the destruction of Sodom and the other Cities of the Plain, which many believed created the Dead Sea, these associations gave these locations layered "meanings which go far beyond their geographical names and which greatly surpass their size and appearance."[294]

Moreover, the expedition took place at a unique moment in history, at the intersection between religious conviction and the scientific method. The questions posed by mid-nineteenth-century explorers in Palestine were attempts to use scientific technologies to prove the veracity of Bible stories. Earlier explorers felt no need to prove what was written in Scripture, and later explorers separated the religious need to identify biblical sites from the scientific imperative to analyze data without a preconceived agenda. But at mid-century, "the Dead Sea and the entire Jordan Valley formed not only a test case, but probably *the* test case" of the attempt to reconcile science and religion.[295]

Lynch's persistent highlighting of the religious element in the Palestine expedition by describing each phase of the journey in terms of its religious significance obscured the expedition's scientific contributions. His popular 1849 book argued that the cataclysm caused by God's wrath destroyed the Cities of the Plain and created the Dead Sea, a popular view as evidenced by the book's multiple printings. But the official report of the expedition, printed in 1852 under Lynch's supervision, contains a geological analysis written by Dr. Anderson that explicitly contradicts Lynch's earlier position by asserting that the volcanic action or fissure that caused the Dead Sea depression happened millions of years ago. The official report separated science from religion—and received praise for doing so.

Lynch's interest in the Jordan River as an alternate trade route to India continued, with W. A. Allen, a British naval engineer, who in 1855 proposed directing Mediterranean waters across Palestine to the Sea of Galilee. He hypothesized that this would set off a chain reaction that would result in the Dead Sea overflowing its southern boundary and connecting to the Red Sea. It was a less expensive alternative to a canal at Suez. This line of reasoning persisted well into the 1880s.[296] Then, in the twentieth century, talk resurfaced of a canal connecting the Dead Sea to the Red Sea as a way of "saving" the Dead Sea. Lynch's map of the Dead Sea, especially the careful depth measurements crisscrossing the lake diagonally, proved invaluable in the distant future, showing up on others' maps of Palestine in the coming decades. Geologists still use them today for comparison in lake levels.

Today, it is easy to dismiss the Palestine expedition as a quaint, more or less forgotten bit of history. This is especially the case because the Civil War soon derailed any plans or fantasies of a more substantial American involvement in Palestine at that time. Still, in the late nineteenth century, all sorts of people—religious leaders, biblical archaeologists, consular officials, and legislators—entertained visions of religious imperialism with the United States redeeming Palestine for American Protestants. Though mostly forgotten today, those who wanted to strengthen the behind-the-scenes involvement of America in Palestine's destiny often cited Lynch's expedition.

Another hundred years would pass before America again took up a role in the territorial politics of the Middle East.

Acknowledgments

I would like to express my gratitude to the New York Public Library, which granted me a short-term fellowship to research in their collections. Many thanks to Dr. Barbara A. Porter, Dr. Christopher A. Tuttle, and other members of the staff at the American Center of Oriental Research in Amman, Jordan, who first encouraged my interest in William Francis Lynch. Also to Claire Gerus, my agent, and James Jayo, my editor at Lyons Press, for agreeing that this is a story that deserves a narrative. As always, I appreciate my daughter, Amber Lea Clark, and my mother, Rose M. Usry, who listen to my ideas and read drafts of my manuscripts.

Endnotes

1   *Square-rigged* is a general term that describes a vessel with large sails that hang from yards attached to a mast. Technically, the *Supply* was ship-rigged because it had three masts; not all sailing vessels were ships. Some were called *barques, brigs, yawls, xebecs,* or other terms, depending upon the configuration of the sails and masts.

2   William Francis Lynch, *Narrative of the United States' Expedition to the River Jordan and the Dead Sea* (Philadelphia: Lea and Blanchard, 1849), 16. Lynch also published a detailed final report about the voyage: *Official Report of the United States' Expedition to Explore the Dead Sea and the River Jordan* (Baltimore: John Murphy & Co., 1852).

3   Lynch, *Narrative,* 117.

4   Ibid., 117.

5   William F. Lynch, *Naval Life; Or, Observations Afloat and on Shore: The Midshipman* (New York: Charles Schribner, 1851), 84.

6   Andrew C. A. Jampoler, *Sailors in the Holy Land: The 1848 American Expedition to the Dead Sea and the Search for Sodom and Gomorrah* (Annapolis, MD: Naval Institute Press, 2005), xvi.

7   "William Francis Lynch (1801–1865)," The Latin Library, accessed April 30, 2012, http://www.thelatinlibrary.com/chron/civilwarnotes/lynch.html.

8   Lynch, *Narrative,* 13.

9   Neil Asher Silberman, *Digging for God and Country: Exploration, Archeology, and the Secret Struggle for the Holy Land, 1799–1917* (New York: Knopf, 1982), 52–3.

10   John Y. Mason to William Francis Lynch, 11 Nov. 1847.

11   Silberman, *Digging for God and Country,* 51–52.

12   Ibid., 7.

13 Palestine, under Ottoman Rule, was not a province to itself, though the name was often used informally to refer to the region. In Lynch's era, Palestine was divided into three administrative units, with Acre assigned to the Beirut province. The Dead Sea region was essentially beyond Ottoman control during this period. See Gideon Biger, *The Boundaries of Modern Palestine, 1840–1947* (New York: Routledge/Curzon, 2004).

14 Muhammad is also sometimes translated from Arabic as Mehmed or Mehme.

15 Hiam Goren, *Dead Sea Level: Science, Exploration and Imperial Interests in the Near East* (London: I. B. Tauris, 2011), 43–44.

16 Silberman, *Digging for God and Country*, 37–41, 47.

17 Edward Robinson and Eli Smith, *Biblical Researches in Palestine, Mount Sinai, and Arabia Petraea. 3 Vol. 1841*, vol. 1 (Boston: Crocker and Brewster, 1841), 41–45.

18 David H. Finnie, *Pioneers East: The Early American Experience in the Middle East* (Cambridge, MA: Harvard University Press, 1967), 269.

19 *New York Herald*, 13 November 1847.

20 Goren, *Dead Sea Level*, 207–22.

21 Edward Robinson, "Depression of the Dead Sea Valley and the Jordan Valley," *Bibliotheca Sacra* 5, no. 9 (1848): 397–409.

22 I Kings 18:38; Lynch, *Narrative*, 118.

23 Jampoler, *Sailors in the Holy Land*, xv, xvi, 1.

24 Hilton Obenzinger, "Holy Land Travel and the American Covenant the Century Palestine in the Settler-Colonial Imagination," *Jerusalem Quarterly*, February 2003, 41–48. Accessed October 29, 2011, http://www.jerusalemquarterly .org/ViewArticle.aspx?id=155.

25 Henry Clay Trumbull, "An Illustrator of the Fifth Gospel: Dr. William M. Thomson," *The Biblical World* 20, no. 5 (1902): 380–84, doi:10.1086/473071.

26 I Kings 18:38; Lynch, *Narrative*, 118.

27 Edward P. Montague, ed., *Narrative of the Late Expedition to the Dead Sea. From a Diary by One of the Party, Edited by Edward P. Montague, With Incidents and Adventures from the Time of the Sailing of the Expedition in November, 1847, Till the Return of the Same in December, 1848* (Philadelphia: Carey and Hart, 1849), 84.

28 Lynch, *Naval Life*, 9.

29 Stephen Howarth, *To Shining Sea: A History of the United States Navy, 1775–1998* (Norman: University of Oklahoma Press, 1999), 130.

30 Auguste Levasseur, *Lafayette in America in 1824 and 1825. Or, Journal of a Voyage to the United States.* Translated by John Davidson Godman, vol. 2 (Philadelphia: Carey and Lea, 1829), 258–259.

31 Frances Leigh Williams, *Matthew Fontaine Maury: Scientist of the Sea* (New Brunswick, N.J.: Rutgers University Press, 1963), 49.

32 Simon Winchester, *Atlantic: Great Sea Battles, Heroic Discoveries, Titanic Storms, and a Vast Ocean of a Million Stories* (New York: Harper Collins, 2010), 132–33.

33 Howarth, *To Shining Sea*, 142; John H. Schroeder, *Shaping a Maritime Empire: The Commercial and Diplomatic Role of the American Navy, 1829–1861* (Westport, CT: Greenwood Press, 1985), 33.

34 Charles Wilkes, U.S.N., *Narrative of the United States's Exploring Expedition: During the Years 1838, 1839, 1840, 1842* (London: Whittaker and Co., 1844), 362.

35 Howarth, *To Shining Sea*, 144.

36 Herman J. Viola and Carolyn Margolis, eds., *Magnificent Voyagers: The U.S. Exploring Expedition, 1838–1842* (Washington, D.C.: Smithsonian Institution Press, 1985), 7.

37 Howarth, *To Shining Sea*, 146.

38 Richard Warner Van Alstyne, *The Rising American Empire* (New York: W.W. Norton, 1974), 1.

39 Howarth, *To Shining Sea*, 149.

40 Schroeder, *Shaping a Maritime Empire*, 9.

41 Robert E. May, *Manifest Destiny's Underworld: Filibustering in Antebellum America* (Chapel Hill: University of North Carolina Press, 2002), 20.

42 Amy S. Greenberg, *Manifest Manhood and the Antebellum American Empire* (Cambridge, UK: Cambridge University Press, 2005), 20.

43 Ibid., 17.

44 Jampoler, *Sailors in the Holy Land*, 39; Vincent Ponko Jr., *Ships, Seas, and Scientists: U.S. Naval Exploration and Discovery in the Nineteenth Century* (Annapolis, MD: Naval Institute Press, 1974), 36.

45　Montague, *Narrative of the Late Expedition to the Dead Sea*, 125.

46　Lynch, *Narrative*, 120.

47　Montague, *Narrative of the Late Expedition to the Dead Sea*, 131.

48　Lynch, *Narrative*, 119.

49　John Davis, *The Landscape of Belief: Encountering the Holy Land in Nineteenth-Century American Art and Culture* (Princeton, NJ: Princeton University Press, 1998), 37.

50　Michael B. Oren, *Power, Faith, and Fantasy: America in the Middle East, 1776 to the Present* (New York: W.W. Norton & Co., 2007), 75.

51　Ibid., 74.

52　Weld Allen Gardner, *Our Navy and the Barbary Corsairs* (Boston: Houghton, Mifflin and Company, 1905), 288; William Shaler, *Sketches of Algiers: Political, Historical, and Civil* (Boston: Cummings and Hillard, 1826), 38.

53　Oren, *Power, Faith, and Fantasy*, 74.

54　*Niles Weekly Register*, 15 April 1815.

55　Allen, *Our Navy and the Barbary Corsairs*, 295

56　Oren, *Power, Faith, and Fantasy*, 76.

57　Montague, *Narrative of the Late Expedition to the Dead Sea*, 134.

58　Oren, *Power, Faith, and Fantasy*, 46; Edward W. Said, *Orientalism* (New York: Pantheon Books, 1978), 94

59　Oren, *Power, Faith, and Fantasy*, 53.

60　Ibid., 54.

61　Lynch, *Narrative*, 72.

62　Ibid., 73.

63　Ibid., 76.

64　Ibid., 77.

65　John Lloyd Stephens, *Incidents of Travel in the Russian and Turkish Empires*, vol. 1. (London: Bentley, 1839), 227.

66　Jampoler, *Sailors in the Holy Land*, 103.

67　Lynch, *Narrative*, 106.

68　Ibid., 77.

69　Kark, *American Consuls in the Holy Land*, 241.

70　Lynch, *Narrative*, 123.

71　Palestine, under Ottoman Rule, was not a province to itself, though the name was often used informally to refer to the region. In Lynch's era, Palestine was divided into three different administrative units, with Acre assigned to the Beirut province. The Dead Sea region was essentially beyond Ottoman control during this period. See Gideon Biger, *The Boundaries of Modern Palestine, 1840-1947* (New York: Routledge/Curzon, 2004).

72 Lynch, *Narrative*, 123.
73 Ibid., 125.
74 Ibid., 125.
75 Robert E. Rook, *The 150th Anniversary of the United States Expedition to Explore the Dead Sea and the River Jordan* (Amman, Jordan: American Center of Oriental Research, 1998), 15.
76 Jampoler, *Sailors in the Holy Land*, 119.
77 Lynch translated the sheikh's name as 'Akil Aga el Hasseé. Other authors have translated it as Akîel Agha (Mary Eliza Rogers, 1865), Akeeli Aga el Hhâsi (James Finn, 1878); Aqil Aga al-Hasi (Alexander Scholch, 1984).
78 Lynch, *Narrative*, 129.
79 Ibid., 130.
80 Ibid., 133.
81 Lt. Molyneux, "Expedition to the Jordan and the Dead Sea," *Journal of the Royal Geographical Society of London* 18 (1848): 104–5.
82 Lynch, *Narrative*, 135.
83 Ibid., 140.
84 Lynch called the fortress Abelin instead of 'Ibillin. The village was located midway between Acre and Turan.
85 Lynch, *Narrative*, 140.
86 Ibid., 146.
87 Ibid., 142.
88 Ibid., 143.
89 Ibid., 150.
90 Rook, *The 150th Anniversary*, 14–15.
91 Lynch, *Narrative*, 152.
92 Ibid., 153.
93 Burke O. Long, *Imagining the Holy Land: Maps, Models, and Fantasy Travels* (Bloomington: Indiana University Press, 2003), 2.
94 Lynch, *Narrative*, 153.

95 Yehoshua Ben-Arieh, *The Rediscovery of the Holy Land in the Nineteenth Century* (Jerusalem: Magnes Press, Hebrew University, 1979), 102.

96 Lynch, *Narrative*, 157.

97 Ibid., 162.

98 Ibid., 162

99 Montague, *Narrative of the Late Expedition to the Dead Sea*, 149.

100 Lynch, *Narrative*, 162.

101 Naomi Shepherd, *The Zealous Intruders: The Western Rediscovery of Palestine* (San Francisco: Harper & Row, 1987), 52; Ben-Arieh, *The Rediscovery of the Holy Land in the Nineteenth Century*, 32; Goren, *Dead Sea Level*, 139–140.

102 Jean-Louis Burckhardt, *Travels in Syria and the Holy Land* (London: Association for Promoting the Discovery of the Interior Parts of Africa, 1822), 428.

103 Edward Daniel Clarke, *Travels in Various Countries of Europe, Asia, and Africa*, second ed. (London: T. Cadell and W. David, 1813), 585–6.

104 Burckhardt, *Travels in Syria and the Holy Land*, vi.

105 Alexander William Kinglake, *Eothen: Traces of Travel Brought Home from the East, 1849*, 98.

106 Kinglake, *Eothen*, 97.

107 Robinson, "Depression of the Dead Sea Valley and the Jordan Valley," 399–400.

108 Ibid., 404–5.

109 Carl Ritter, *Comparative Geography of Palestine and the Sinaitic Peninsula*, Vol. 2, (Edinburg: T & T Clark, 1866), 260.

110 Lynch, *Narrative*, 172.

111 Ibid., 169.

112 Ibid., 173.

113 Ibid., 171.

114 Ibid., 168.

115 Ibid., 526.

116 Ibid., 169.

117 Ibid., 174.

118 Ibid., 174.

119 Molyneux, "Expedition to the Jordan and the Dead Sea."

120 Lynch, *Narrative*, 175.

121 Ibid., 176.

122 Montague, *Narrative of the Late Expedition to the Dead Sea*, 158.

123 Lynch, *Narrative*, 178.

124 Ibid., 178.

125 Janpoler, *Sailors in the Holy Land*, 138.

126 Lynch, *Narrative*, 185.

127 Ibid., 195.

128 Alexander Scholch, "The Decline of Local Power in Palestine after 1856: The Case of Aqil Aga," *Die Welt Des Islams* 23, no. 1/4 (1984): 462, doi:10.2307/1570684.

129 Ibid., 462–64.

130 Lynch, *Narrative*, 196.

131 Ibid., 254.

132 Ibid., 256.

133 Ibid., 214.

134 Ibid., 255–56.

135 Ibid., 256.

136 Ibid., 260.

137 Ibid., 260–61.

138 Ibid., 281.

139 Montague, *Narrative of the Late Expedition to the Dead Sea*, 176.

140 Ibid., 176.

141 "Pilgrimage of the Greek Christians to the Waters of the Jordan," in *Littell's Living Age*, comp. E. Littell, vol. 14 (Boston: E. Littell & Co, 1847), 27.

142 Jampoler, *Sailors in the Holy Land*, 151–52.

143 Montague, *Narrative of the Late Expedition to the Dead Sea*, 177.

144 Today, however, the baptismal site on the east bank, called Bethany-beyond-the-Jordan, is in Jordan while the one on the other side, Qasr al-Yahud, is in the West Bank, part of Israel. Following the peace treaty between Jordan and Israel in 1994, Jordan began excavations. To date, archaeologists have uncovered more than twenty churches, caves, and baptismal pools, some dating back to the Roman and Byzantine eras.

145 Ritter, *Comparative Geography*, 287.

146 Montague, *Narrative of the Late Expedition to the Dead Sea*, 179.

147 Ibid., 180.

148 Henry Maundrell, *A Journey From Alepo to Jerusalem at Easter 1697. Fifth Edit. In Which Is Now Added an Account of the Author's Journey to the Banks of Euphrates at Beer and to the Country of Mesopotamia* (Oxford, UK: Theater, 1732), 85.

149 Gordon S. Wood, *Empire of Liberty: A History of the Early Republic, 1789–1815* (New York: Oxford University Press, 2009), 576.

150 Robert Steele, ed., *Medieval Lore: An Epitome of the Science, Geography, Animal and Plant Folk-lore and Myth of the Middle Age: Being Classified Gleanings from the Encyclopedia of Bartholomew Anglicus on the Properties of Things*, (London: Elliot Stock, 1893), 70.

151 Thomas Fuller, *A Pisgah-sight of Palestine and the Confines Thereof: With the History of the Old and New Testament Acted Thereon* (London: John Williams, 1662), 596.

152 Lynch, *Narrative*, 269.

153 Ibid., 269.

154 Ibid., 271.

155 Ibid., 272.

156 Ulrich Jasper Seetzen, *A Brief Account of the Countries Adjoining the Lake of Tiberias, the Jordan, and the Dead Sea* (London: Palestine Association of London, 1810), 40.

157 Ibid., 40.

158 Ibid., 44.

159 Ibid., 45.

160 Goren, *Dead Sea Level*, 195.

161 Ibid., 159.

162 J. D. Paxton, *Letters from Palestine: Written during a Residence There in the Years 1836, 7, and 8* (London: Charles Tilt, 1839), 162–63.

163 Robinson and Smith, *Biblical Researches*, 670–71.

164 Goren, *Dead Sea Level*, 195.

165 Ibid., 196.

166 Ibid., 205.

167 Ibid., 189.

168 Ibid., 158.

169 Ibid., 167.

170 Ibid., 214.

171 Quoted in Ibid., 210.

172 Ibid., 110–11.

173 Quoted in Ibid., 213.

174 Ibid., 223.

175 Ibid., 214.

176 Ibid., 218.
177 Ibid., 218–20.
178 Edward Robinson, "Depression of the Dead Sea and of the Jordan Valley," *Journal of the Royal Geographical Society of London* 18 (1848): 77–88, especially 87; "Depression of the Dead Sea Valley and the Jordan Valley," *Bibliotheca Sacra* 5, no. 9 (1848): 397–409; "Researches in Palestine," *Bibliotheca Sacra* 1 (February 1843): 9–89; "The Dead Sea Expedition," *Bibliotheca Sacra* 5, no. 20 (1848): 764–70.
179 Goren, *Dead Sea Level*, 222.
180 Lynch, *Narrative*, 273.
181 Ibid., 274.
182 Robinson and Smith, *Biblical Researches*, 222.
183 Lynch, *Narrative*, 275
184 William Hughes, *The Illuminated Atlas of Scripture Geography: A Series of Maps, Delineating the Physical and Historical Features in the Geography of Palestine and the Adjacent Countries* (London: Knight, 1840), 36.
185 Jeremiah 51:43.
186 Lynch, *Narrative*, 274.
187 Ibid, 274.
188 Ibid., 277.
189 Ibid., 279.
190 Barbara Kreiger, *Living Waters: Myth, History, and Politics of the Dead Sea* (New York: Continuum, 1988), 32–3.
191 Shepherd, *The Zealous Intruders*, 14.
192 Burckhardt, *Travels in Syria and the Holy Land*, 6.
193 Davis, *The Landscape of Belief*, 30; Silberman, *Digging for God and Country*, 54.
194 Robinson and Smith, *Biblical Researches*, 374.
195 Lynch, *Narrative*, 288.
196 Kreiger, *Living Waters*, 96.
197 1 Samuel 24:2.
198 Robinson and Smith, *Biblical Researches*, 44.
199 Yolande Jones, "British Military Surveys of Palestine and Syria 1840–1841," *The Cartography Journal* 10, no. 1 (1973): 30.
200 Jampoler, *Sailors in the Holy Land*, 255.
201 Lynch, *Narrative*, 294.
202 Ibid., 295.

203 Ibid., 295.

204 Robinson and Smith, *Biblical Researches*, 204–06.

205 Ibid., 208–9.

206 Lynch, *Narrative*, 305

207 Ibid., 305.

208 Flavius Josephus, *Jewish Antiquities* (Ware, Hertfordshire: Watsworth Editions, 2006), 29.

209 Lynch, *Narrative*, 307.

210 Lynch, *Official Report*, 181.

211 Lynch, *Narrative*, 309.

212 Ibid., 312.

213 Ibid., 313.

214 Ibid., 314.

215 Ibid., 315.

216 Ibid., 317.

217 Ibid., 335.

218 Ibid., 336.

219 David Grossman, *Rural Arab Demography and Early Jewish Settlement in Palestine: Distribution and Population Density during the Late Ottoman and Early Mandate Periods* (New Brunswick, NJ: Transaction Publishers, 2010), 49–50.

220 Barbara Kreiger, *The Dead Sea: Myth, History, and Politics* (Hanover, NH: University Press of New England, 1997), 78.

221 Lynch, *Narrative*, 324.

222 Ibid., 328.

223 Ibid., 322.

224 Ibid., 323-24.

225 Ibid., 323.

226 Ibid., 324.

227 Ibid., 325.

228 Ibid., 325.

229 Ibid., 337.

230 Ritter, *Comparative Geography*, 121.

231 Ibid., 122.

232 Lynch, *Narrative*, 344.

233 Ibid., 345.

234 Ibid., 346.

235 Ibid., 346.

236 Ibid., 348.

237 Ritter, *Comparative Geography*, 76.

238 Lynch, *Narrative*, 352.

239 Ibid., 354–55.

240 Ibid., 358.

241 Maundrell, *A Journey from Alepo to Jerusalem*, 49.

242 Lynch, *Narrative*, 368.

243 Ibid., 362.

244 Ibid., 363.

245 Ibid., 365.

246 Ibid., 376.

247 Montague, *Narrative of the Late Expedition to the Dead Sea*, 231.

248 Lynch, *Narrative*, 378–79.

249 Ibid., 380.

250 Ibid., 381

251 Ibid., 383.

252 Ibid., 384.

253 Hilton Obenzinger, *American Palestine: Melville, Twain, and the Holy Land Mania* (Princeton, NJ: Princeton University Press, 1999), 55; Davis, *The Landscape of Belief*, 33.

254 Lynch, *Narrative*, 386.

255 Ibid., 391.

256 Sherman Lieber, *Mystics and Missionaries: The Jews in Palestine, 1799–1840* (Salt Lake City: University of Utah Press, 1992), 25.

257 Arnold Blumberg, *Zion before Zionism, 1838–1880* (Jerusalem: Devora Publishing, 2007), 4–6; Lieber, *Mystics and Missionaries*, 24.

258 Robinson and Smith, *Biblical Researches*, 326.

259 Lynch, *Narrative*, 398.

260 Ibid., 398.

261 Menashe Har-El, *Golden Jerusalem* (Jerusalem: Gefen, 2004), 54.

262 Blumberg, *Zion before Zionism*, 12.

263 Ibid., 21–22.

264 William M. Thomson, *The Land and the Book: Or, Biblical Illustrations Drawn from the Manners and Customs, the Scenes and Scenery, of the Holy Land*, vol. 1 (New York: Harpers and Brothers, 1888), 24; Long, *Imagining the Holy Land*, 135.

265 Long, *Imagining the Holy Land*, 133–34.

266 Obenzinger, *American Palestine*, 31–2, 105.

267 Lynch, *Narrative*, 360.

268 Bayard Taylor, *The Lands of the Saracen: Or, Pictures of Palestine, Asia Minor, Sicily and Spain* (New York: G.P. Putnam's Sons, 1873), 52; Obenzinger, *American Palestine*, 55.

269 Lynch, *Narrative*, 397.

270 Montague, *Narrative of the Late Expedition to the Dead Sea*, 404.

271 Obenzinger, *American Palestine*, 55.

272 Lynch, *Narrative*, 405.

273 Robinson and Smith, *Biblical Researches*, 336.

274 Brian Yothers, *The Romance of the Holy Land in American Travel Writing, 1790–1876* (Aldershot, Hants, England: Ashgate, 2007), 20, 25; Long, *Imagining the Holy Land*, 132–3.

275 Lynch, *Narrative*, 409.

276 Ibid., 409.

277 Ibid., 415.

278 Ibid., 415.

279 Lynch, *Official Report*, 43; Goren, *Dead Sea Level*, 265.

280 Goren, *Dead Sea Level*, 484.

281 Lynch, *Narrative*, 439.

282 Ibid., 439.

283 Ibid., 477.

284 Ibid., 477.

285 Ibid., 483.

286 Ibid., 502.

287 Janpoler, *Sailors in the Holy Land*, 241.

288 David Haward Bain, *Bitter Waters: America's Forgotten Naval Mission to the Dead Sea* (New York: Overlook Press, 2011), 319; Janpoler, *Sailors in the Holy Land*, 257.

289 Bain, *Bitter Waters*, 291.

290 Scholch, "The Decline of Local Power, 471.

291 Quoted in Janpoler, *Sailors in the Holy Land*, 259.

292 Bane, *Bitter Waters*, 291.

293 Janpoler, *Sailors in the Holy Land*, 13.

294 Goren, *Dead Sea Level*, 267.

295 Ibid., 267.

296 Shepherd, *The Zealous Intruders*, 87-88.

Bibliography

Primary Sources

Buckingham, James Silk. *Travels in Palestine, through the Countries of Bashan and Gilead, East of the River Jordan.* Vol. 2. London: Longman, Hurst, Rees, Orme, and Brown, 1821.

Burckhardt, Jean Louis. *Travels in Syria and the Holy Land.* London: Association for Promoting the Discovery of the Interior Parts of Africa, 1822.

Carne, John. *Letters from the East Written during a Recent Tour through Turkey, Egypt, Arabien, The Holy Land, Syria, and Greece.* London: H. Colburn, 1826.

Clarke, Edward Daniel. *Travels in Various Countries of Europe, Asia, and Africa.* London: T. Cadell and W. David, 1813.

Conder, Claude Reignier. *Tent Work in Palestine: A Record of Discovery and Adventure.* New York: D. Appleton & Co., 1878.

Francis' Metallic Life-boat Company. New York: W.C. Bryant & Co., 1852.

Fuller, Thomas. *A Pisgah-sight of Palestine and the Confines Thereof: With the History of the Old and New Testament Acted Thereon.* London: John Williams, 1662.

Hughes, William. *The Illuminated Atlas of Scripture Geography: A Series of Maps, Delineating the Physical and Historical Features in the Geography of Palestine and the Adjacent Countries.* London: Knight, 1840.

Irby, Charles Leonard, and James Mangles. *Travels in Egypt and Nubia, Syria, and the Holy Land; including a Journey round the Dead Sea, and through the Country East of the Jordan.* London: John Murray, 1844.

Josephus, Flavius. *Jewish Antiquities.* Edited by Brian McGing. Ware, Hertfordshire: Watsworth Editions, 2006.

Kinglake, Alexander William. *Eothen: Traces of Travel Brought Home from the East.* New York: G.P. Putnam, 1849.

Levasseur, Auguste. *Lafayette in America in 1824 and 1825, Or, Journal of a Voyage to the United States.* Translated by John Davidson Godman. Vol. 2. Philadelphia: Carey and Lea, 1829.

Lynch, William Francis. *Narrative of the United States' Expedition to the River Jordan and the Dead Sea.* Philadelphia: Lea and Blanchard, 1849.

———. *Naval Life; Or, Observations Afloat and on Shore: The Midshipman.* New York: Charles Scribner, 1851.

———. *Official Report of the United States' Expedition to Explore the Dead Sea and the River Jordan.* Baltimore: John Murphy & Co., 1852.

Maundrell, Henry. *A Journey from Alepo to Jerusalem at Easter 1697. Fifth Edit. In Which Is Now Added an Account of the Author's Journey to the Banks of Euphrates at Beer and to the Country of Mesopotamia.* Oxford, UK: Theater, 1732.

Molyneux, Lt. "Expedition to the Jordan and the Dead Sea." *Journal of the Royal Geographical Society of London* 18 (1848): 104–30.

Montague, Edward P., ed. *Narrative of the Late Expedition to the Dead Sea. From a Diary by One of the Party, Edited by Edward P. Montague, With Incidents and Adventures from the Time of the Sailing of the Expedition in November, 1847, Till the Return of the Same in December, 1848.* Philadelphia: Carey and Hart, 1849.

Paxton, J. D. *Letters from Palestine: Written during a Residence There in the Years 1836, 7, and 8.* London: Charles Tilt, 1839.

"Pilgrimage of the Greek Christians to the Waters of the Jordan," in *Littell's Living Age,* comp. E. Littell, vol. 14. Boston: E. Littell & Co, 1847.

Robinson, Edward. *Biblical Researches in Palestine.* New York: Price & Reed, 1842.

———. "Depression of the Dead Sea and of the Jordan Valley." *Journal of the Royal Geographical Society of London* 18 (1848): 77–88.

———. "Depression of the Dead Sea Valley and the Jordan Valley." *Bibliotheca Sacra* 5, no. 9 (1848): 397–409.

———. *Physical Geography of the Holy Land.* Boston: Crocker and Brewster, 1865.

Robinson, Edward, and Eli Smith. *Biblical Researches in Palestine, Mount Sinai, and Arabia Petraea. 3 Vol. 1841.* Vol. 1. Boston: Crocker and Brewster, 1841.

Seetzen, Ulrich Jasper. *A Brief Account of the Countries Adjoining the Lake of Tiberias, the Jordan, and the Dead Sea.* London: Palestine Association of London, 1810.

Shaler, William. *Sketches of Algiers, Political, Historical, and Civil.* Boston: Cummings and Hillard, 1826.

Spencer, J. A. *The East: Sketches of Travel in Egypt and the Holy Land.* New York: G. P. Putnam, 1850.

Stephens, John Lloyd. *Incidents of Travel in Egypt, Arabia Petræa, and the Holy Land: With a Map and Engravings.* New York: Harper & Brothers, 1838.

———. *Incidents of Travel in the Russian and Turkish Empires.* London, 1839.

Taylor, Bayard. *The Lands of the Saracen: Or, Pictures of Palestine, Asia Minor, Sicily and Spain.* New York: G.P. Putnam's Sons, 1873.

Thomson, William M. *The Land and the Book: Or, Biblical Illustrations Drawn from the Manners and Customs, the Scenes and Scenery, of the Holy Land.* New York: Harper & Brothers, 1888.

Van De Velde, Carl Wille Meredith. *Narrative of a Journey through Syria and Palestine in 1851 and 1852.* Edinburg: W. Blackwood, 1854.

Washington, John. "Sketch of the Progress of Geography during the Past Year, and of the Labours of the Geographical Society 1836–7." *Journal of the Royal Geographical Society* 7 (1837): 183.

Wilkes, Charles, USN. *Narrative of the United States's Exploring Expedition: During the Years 1838, 1839, 1840, 1842.* London: Whittaker and Co., 1844.

Unpublished Papers

"Letters and Reports from Lieutenant William Francis Lynch," National Archives

"Letters Secretary of the Navy to Officers 1798–1868," National Archives microfilm file M149, Vols. 40, 41, and 42.

Matthew Fontaine Maury Papers, Library of Congress

William Francis Lynch file, Navy Department Library

Secondary Sources

Aiken, Edwin J. *Scriptural Geography: Portraying the Holy Land.* London: I. B. Tauris, 2009.

Allen, Gardner Weld. *Our Navy and the Barbary Corsairs.* Boston: Houghton, Mifflin and Company, 1905.

Allen, William. *The Dead Sea, a New Route to India.* London: Longman, Brown, Green, and Longmans, 1855.

Bain, David Haward. *Bitter Waters: America's Forgotten Naval Mission to the Dead Sea.* New York: Overlook Press, 2011.

Bannister, J. T. *A Survey of the Holy Land: Its Geography, History, and Destiny.* London: Binns and Goodwin, 1844.

Ben-Arieh, Yehoshua. "The Geological Exploration of the Holy Land." *Palestine Exploration Quarterly Statement* 104 (1972): 81–92.

———. "Pioneer Scientific Exploration in the Holy Land at the Beginning of the Nineteenth Century." *Terrae Incognitae* 4 (1972): 95–110.

———. *The Rediscovery of the Holy Land in the Nineteenth Century.* Jerusalem: Magnes Press, Hebrew University, 1979.

———. "William F. Lynch's Expedition to the Dead Sea, 1847–48." *Prologue,* 1973, 15–21.

Blumberg, Arnold. *Zion before Zionism, 1838–1880.* Jerusalem: Devora Publishing, 2007.

Bryson, Thomas A. *American Diplomatic Relations with the Middle East, 1784–1975: A Survey.* Metuchen, NJ: Scarecrow Press, 1977.

Cherry, Conrad. *God's New Israel: Religious Interpretations of American Destiny.* Englewood Cliffs, NJ: Prentice-Hall, 1971.

Costello, Con. *Ireland and the Holy Land: An Account of Irish Links with the Levant from the Earliest Times.* Dublin: C. Goodliffe Neal, 1974.

Davis, John. *The Landscape of Belief: Encountering the Holy Land in Nineteenth-century American Art and Culture.* Princeton, NJ: Princeton University Press, 1998.

Eriksen, Erik Olaf. "Christopher Costigan (1810–1835): Irish Explorer of the Dead Sea." *Holy Land,* 1985, 41–49.

———. "The Illness of Christopher Costigan—A Case of Heat Stroke." *Dublin Historical Record* 39 (June 1986): 82–85.

Field, James A. *America and the Mediterranean World, 1776–1882.* Princeton, NJ: Princeton University Press, 1969.

———. *From Gibraltar to the Middle East: America and the Mediterranean World, 1776–1882.* Chicago: Imprint Publications, 1991.

Finnie, David H. *Pioneers East: The Early American Experience in the Middle East.* Cambridge, MA: Harvard University Press, 1967.

Goren, Haim. *Dead Sea Level: Science, Exploration and Imperial Interests in the Near East.* London: I. B. Tauris, 2011.

———. "Sacred, but Not Surveyed: Nineteenth-century Surveys of Palestine." *Imago Mundi* 54, no. 1 (2002): 87–110. doi:10.1080/03085690208592960.

Grabill, Joseph L. *Protestant Diplomacy and the Near East: Missionary Influence on American Policy, 1810–1927.* Minneapolis: University of Minnesota Press, 1971.

Greenberg, Amy S. *Manifest Manhood and the Antebellum American Empire.* Cambridge, UK: Cambridge University Press, 2005.

Grossman, David. *Rural Arab Demography and Early Jewish Settlement in Palestine: Distribution and Population Density during the Late Ottoman and Early Mandate Periods.* New Brunswick, NJ: Transaction Publishers, 2010.

Har-El, Menashe. *Golden Jerusalem.* Jerusalem: Gefen, 2004.

Horowitz, Aharon, and Kiva Flexer. *The Jordan Rift Valley.* New York: Taylor and Francis, 2001.

Howarth, Stephen. *To Shining Sea: A History of the United States Navy, 1775–1998.* Norman: University of Oklahoma Press, 1999.

Howe, Daniel Walker. *What Hath God Wrought: The Transformation of America, 1815–1848.* New York: Oxford University Press, 2007.

Jampoler, Andrew C. A. *Sailors in the Holy Land: The 1848 American Expedition to the Dead Sea and the Search for Sodom and Gomorrah.* Annapolis, MD: Naval Institute Press, 2005.

Jones, Yolande. "British Military Surveys of Palestine and Syria 1840–1841." *The Cartography Journal* 10, no. 1 (1973): 29–41.

Kark, Ruth. *American Consuls in the Holy Land: 1832–1914.* Jerusalem: Magnes Press, 1994.

Kreiger, Barbara. *The Dead Sea: Myth, History, and Politics.* Hanover, NH: University Press of New England, 1997.

———. *Living Waters: Myth, History, and Politics of the Dead Sea.* New York: Continuum, 1988.

Lieber, Sherman. *Mystics and Missionaries: The Jews in Palestine, 1799–1840.* Salt Lake City: University of Utah Press, 1992.

Long, Burke O. *Imagining the Holy Land: Maps, Models, and Fantasy Travels.* Bloomington: Indiana University Press, 2003.

Masterman, E. W. G. "Explorations in the Dead Sea Valley." *The Biblical World* 25, no. 6 (1905): 407–21. doi:10.1086/473588.

———. "Three Early Explorers in the Dead Sea Valley: Costigan-Molyneux-Lynch." *Palestine Exploration Quarterly Statement* 43 (1911): 12–19.

May, Robert E. *Manifest Destiny's Underworld: Filibustering in Antebellum America.* Chapel Hill: University of North Carolina Press, 2002.

Moore, Maurice George. *An Irish Gentleman, George Henry Moore: His Travel, His Racing, His Politics.* London: T. W. Laurie, 1913.

Moscrop, John James. *Measuring Jerusalem: The Palestine Exploration Fund and British Interests in the Holy Land.* London: Leicester University Press, 2000.

Obenzinger, Hilton. *American Palestine: Melville, Twain, and the Holy Land Mania.* Princeton, NJ: Princeton University Press, 1999.

———. "Holy Land Travel and the American Covenant the Century Palestine in the Settler-Colonial Imagination." *Jerusalem Quarterly,* February 2003, 41–48.

Oren, Michael B. *Power, Faith, and Fantasy: America in the Middle East, 1776 to the Present.* New York: W.W. Norton, 2007.

Parkes, James. *Whose Land? A History of the Peoples of Palestine.* New York: Taplinger, 1971.

Poggendorff, Johann Christian. "On the Difference of Level between the Dead Sea and the Mediterranean." *The Edinburgh New Philosophical Journal* 29 (1840): 96–103.

Ponko, Vincent, Jr. *Ships, Seas, and Scientists; U.S. Naval Exploration and Discovery in the Nineteenth Century.* Annapolis, MD: Naval Institute Press, 1974.

Ritter, Carl. *Comparative Geography of Palestine and the Sinaitic Peninsula.* Vol. 2. Edinburg: T & T Clark, 1866.

Robinson, Edward. "The Dead Sea Expedition." *Bibliotheca Sacra* 5, no. 20 (1848): 764–70.

———. "Researches in Palestine." *Bibliotheca Sacra* 1 (February 1843): 9–89.

Rook, Robert E. *The 150th Anniversary of the United States Expedition to Explore the Dead Sea and the River Jordan.* Amman, Jordan: American Center of Oriental Research, 1998.

Said, Edward W. *Orientalism.* New York: Pantheon Books, 1978.

Scholch, Alexander. "The Decline of Local Power in Palestine after 1856: The Case of Aqil Aga." *Die Welt Des Islams* 23, no. 1/4 (1984): 458–75. doi:10.2307/1570684.

———. "The Democratic Development of Palestine, 1850–1882." *International Journal of Middle East Studies* 17 (1985): 485–505.

———. "European Penetration and the Economic Development of Palestine." In *Studies in the Economic and Social History of Palestine in the Nineteenth and Twentieth Centuries,* 10–87. Oxford, UK: St. Anthony's, 1982.

Schroeder, John Henry. *Shaping a Maritime Empire: The Commercial and Diplomatic Role of the American Navy, 1829–1861.* Westport, CT: Greenwood Press, 1985.

Selcer, Richard F. *Civil War America, 1850 to 1875.* New York: Infobase Publishing, 2006.

Shepherd, Naomi. *The Zealous Intruders: The Western Rediscovery of Palestine.* San Francisco: Harper & Row, 1987.

Silberman, Neil Asher. *Digging for God and Country: Exploration, Archeology, and the Secret Struggle for the Holy Land, 1799–1917.* New York: Knopf, 1982.

Steele, Robert, ed. *Medieval Lore: An Epitome of the Science, Geography, Animal and Plant Folk-lore and Myth of the Middle Age: Being Classified Gleanings from the Encyclopedia of Bartholomew Anglicus on the Properties of Things.* London: Elliot Stock, 1893.

"Stella Maris Carmelite Monastery, Haifa." Stella Maris Carmelite Monastery. Accessed April 30, 2012. http://www.sacred-destinations.com/israel/haifa-stella-maris-carmelite-monastery.htm.

Trumbull, Henry Clay. "An Illustrator of the Fifth Gospel: Dr. William M. Thomson." *The Biblical World* 20, no. 5 (1902): 380–84. doi:10.1086/473071.

Tuchman, Barbara Wertheim. *Bible and Sword: How the British Came to Palestine.* London: Macmillan, 1983.

Van Alstyne, Richard Warner. *The Rising American Empire.* New York: Norton, 1974.

Viola, Herman J., and Carolyn Margolis, eds. *Magnificent Voyagers: The U.S. Exploring Expedition, 1838–1842.* Washington, D.C.: Smithsonian Institution Press, 1985.

Vogel, Lester Irwin. *To See a Promised Land: Americans and the Holy Land in the Nineteenth Century.* University Park: Pennsylvania State University Press, 1993.

"William Francis Lynch (1801–1865)." The Latin Library. Accessed April 30, 2012. http://www.thelatinlibrary.com/chron/civil warnotes/lynch.html.

Williams, Frances Leigh. *Matthew Fontaine Maury: Scientist of the Sea.* New Brunswick, NJ: Rutgers University Press, 1963.

Williams, Jay G. *The Times and Life of Edward Robinson: Connecticut Yankee in King Solomon's Court.* Atlanta, GA: Society of Biblical Literature, 1999.

Winchester, Simon. *Atlantic: Great Sea Battles, Heroic Discoveries, Titanic Storms, and a Vast Ocean of a Million Stories.* New York: Harper Collins, 2010.

Wood, Gordon S. *Empire of Liberty: A History of the Early Republic, 1789–1815.* New York: Oxford University Press, 2009.

Yothers, Brian. *The Romance of the Holy Land in American Travel Writing, 1790–1876.* Aldershot, Hants, England: Ashgate, 2007.

Index